ABCs
of Making Money
Online by Ray Boileau

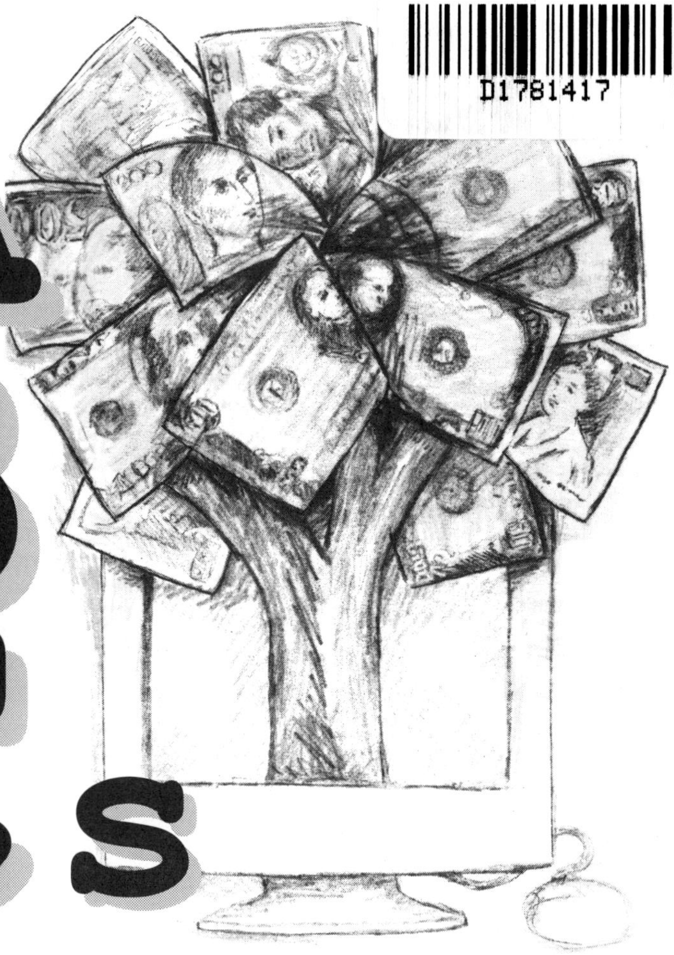

Published by  Hobby House Press
Grantsville, Maryland 21536

Dedication

To general line antiques and collectibles dealers everywhere, many who too often work for 25 cents an hour because they love what they do.

ABC's of Collecting Online has been written to be as accurate as possible. The author, publisher, agents and assignees cannot be held responsible for any error that may occur within the text of this book, nor held responsible for any problems or cumputer viruses that the user may encounter utilizing the Internet or any other online service provider.

Ray Boileau has been involved in the pre-press and printing industry for twenty-five years and was among the first in the 1970s to experiment with computers as a complement to printing, long before desktop publishing was conceived. He currently is a computer consultant who designs Web pages and specializes in Web site implementation.

Ray has also been buying and selling antiques and collectibles for eighteen years. He now works as an antiques dealer offering Internet sales as well as selling through several conventional locations. He has been using or monitoring many of the online auctions since their inceptions.

Additional copies of this book may be purchased at $12.95 (plus postage and handling) from
Hobby House Press, Inc.
1 Corporate Drive
Grantsville, Maryland 21536
1-800-554-1447
or from your favorite bookstore or dealer.
©1999 by Ray Boileau
All rights reserved. No part of this book may be reproduced or utilized in any form or by any means, electronic or mechanical, including photocopying, recording, or by any information storage and retrieval system, without permission in writing from the publisher.
Inquiries should be addressed to
Hobby House Press, Inc., 1 Corporate Drive, Grantsville, Maryland 21536.
Printed in the United States of America
ISBN: 0-87588-555-1

TABLE OF CONTENTS

INTRODUCTION	4
CHAPTER 1 - Opportunities Abound!	7
CHAPTER 2 - The Personal Touch circa 1999	13
CHAPTER 3 - Success Stories	18
CHAPTER 4 - What's In It For Me?	26
CHAPTER 5 - HTML-Dress for Success	29
CHAPTER 6 - Being Seen in All the Right Places	52
CHAPTER 7 - Traditional Sources for Merchandise	58
CHAPTER 8 - Online Sources for Merchandise	73
CHAPTER 9 - Online Tools to Make It Easy	85
CHAPTER 10 - Auction Enhancing Software	101
CHAPTER 11 - Digital Strategies	117
CHAPTER 12 Keeping Records for People Who Hate to Keep Records	122
CHAPTER 13 - To Employ, or not to Employ	126
CHAPTER 14 - Rules and Regulations	132
APPENDIX A	140

Introduction

Every place I go, dealers, retailers, and business owners ask me about using the online auctions. They want to know how to get involved, because they have heard that is not difficult. Some of them are skeptical.

Most of them ask me about eBay™, which is becoming almost a generic term to describe this type of buying and selling. If you learn only one thing from this book, let it be this: while I heartily recommend every dealer to have an online presence, the amount of time it takes to bulk sell items on an online auction must be considered. Your investment in time will be considerable, and you must budget that time to allow for your other activities such as running your shop(s), restocking your booth(s), and attending auctions. If you don't devote much thought to time management now, I guarantee you will have to if you intend to routinely list items with an online auction.

Also remember that eBay™ is not the only place on the Internet to buy and sell, and the Internet is not just about eBay™. As far as online auctions go, eBay™ was first and they are by far the biggest, but there are many others.

During the summer of 1999, I have personally received more eBay™ merchandise with damage that was not mentioned in the description than I received in the previous 3.5 years I have been buying from online auctions. Much of this is due to the inexperience of the sellers using eBay™. eBay™ currently caters to the masses instead of specializing, leaving the door wide open for sellers with little knowledge in certain types of merchandise to sell it anyway.

Some auction sites are beginning to specialize in just antiques and collectibles, or glassware, or pottery, but eBay™ seems to have built such a lead on everyone else that few people frequent these sites. Some reputable sellers and savvy buyers are beginning to deal on these sites because the ratio of high quality merchandise is better, and specialty sites typically don't harbor as many of the con artists and "junk" sellers that seem to congregate around eBay™. A few auction sites make experts available that you can communicate with via e-mail to ask questions about your area of interest. Additionally, the sites that aren't as well known should logically be hiding the best deals if you are buying, simply because the traffic and competition isn't as fierce there. Don't overlook these resources when you're buying. If you decide to sell on these sites, however, know that for now the amount of exposure your item gets will be much less than if you listed on eBay™.

You also don't want to overlook having a Web presence in the form of a business Web site. We will explore the secrets of creating one and attracting people to it. Most people are surprised to find that bringing the people is harder than building a site.

The wealth of information available on the Internet is astounding once you know where to look. From online price guides to recognizing fakes, cyberspace is jammed full of information that will make you a more knowledgeable dealer. While it's true that anybody can post information on the Internet, and everybody has an opinion that may or may not be useful, most of the information is enlightening. Use the Internet to educate yourself—knowledge is power in any business.

I tell everyone, particularly the antiques and collectibles dealers, the same thing. "It is a revolution! It is unbelievable at times! If you are not using the resources available to you on the Internet to supplement your income, you are overlooking what could be the most lucrative market this industry has ever known! Some antiques and collectibles dealers are showing profit margins of 60% online, versus 15-20% (or less) in antique malls. Don't feel badly if you haven't taken the plunge yet, but do it NOW!"

Most of them do. And to a person, they tell me stories about the item they had just about given up on because it had been in their booth or shop for over a year. "I put it on eBay™, and I set the reserve at $150, and before it was over I had $300 for this item!" They look at me with amazement, and I tell them that "this is the difference the Internet can make. The difference is in exposing your merchandise to more people during a seven-day auction than will see it in your mall booth or shop over months, and perhaps years."

To a person, they also tell me it takes more of their time than they expected. In the case of using the online auctions, taking a photo with a digital camera, uploading it, and filling out an online form doesn't sound like much, but believe me it can be. Writing descriptions is tedious for some, and you will probably be surprised how long it takes to answer e-mails, contact high bidders, figure shipping costs, and pack and ship your items. Don't let me lead you into this without telling you there is a time commitment to be made. There is, and it's not to be taken lightly if you expect to be successful. You can use the online auctions to supplement your income rather easily, but if you decide to make a career of it you need to be ready to accept the fact that you must be a small business owner, and with that responsibility you will need certain skills. This book will address not only the online tools available to you, but also the skills you need to be successful.

When used correctly, the Internet is indeed a great tool. While you can't expect everything you try to sell to bring several times what you were hoping for, if you have good quality merchandise you'll do well most of the time. And if you have high-quality, unusual merchandise you'll do very well. Even large furniture pieces, traditionally not sold online due to the cost of shipping, have started to appear and sell for prices that will make almost any dealer happy. I expect this trend to continue with quality players like Sotheby's throwing their hats into the online auction ring.

Don't be fazed by articles you have read about how nobody is making money on the Internet. While that was largely true during the first few years of commercial growth, at this point some ground rules can be established to enhance your chances of success. If you have waited to join the Internet business community, don't fret. All you've done is stand by while the pioneers have pushed forward, many of them becoming casualties. While it may sound impressive to be called a pioneer, as with many of the romanticized stories you've heard about bygone days it was not a wonderful experience for many. Now it is time to learn from recent history and apply the rules those pioneers have taught us. Be sure to read the chapter titled *Success Stories* to get tips from successful sellers in their own words.

By now many of you have already used and mastered the details of buying and selling on the Internet—if you don't feel comfortable with it or have the attitude (as I do) that you can always learn more, I highly recommend my companion book, **The ABCs of Collecting Online**. As for this book, I will show you how to use the traditional methods of finding merchandise, the tricks of retailing, and the Internet experience that will give you the best chance of selling antiques, collectibles, or most anything else profitably. The principles outlined here can be used to sell any kind of merchandise. While much of the book will focus on the building of a successful Internet antiques business, retailers, hobbyists, and any and all of you will surely benefit also. The Internet is a big place, and there is room for all of us!

CHAPTER 1
Opportunities Abound!

The Internet has opened up doors and opportunities that have never before been available to the average person. If you already have a computer, an Internet connection, and are willing to study and learn, you can open a business online for nothing more than your time! That's right—no trip to the bank for a business loan, no putting up your life savings, no borrowing from relatives (which was never a good idea anyway)—absolutely positively free! This book will show you how to have a well-rounded Internet business even if you are starting from scratch, and while I will focus on the antiques and collectibles business, you can apply the rules to selling any type of merchandise you enjoy dealing in. We will explore all of these opportunities in greater detail during later chapters, but here's an overview of what you can expect. This is not rocket science, and with a little patience you will master these tasks and marvel at how easy it is.

Most Internet Service Providers offer a small amount of space on one of their servers as part of your monthly Internet access fee. You can upload files to this server from your computer, and these files become the building blocks of a Web page. To format these blocks into something that will display in a browser window, you can spend about $100 for a web authoring software program like Microsoft Front Page or Adobe PageMill. These software packages are fairly easy to use and make creating Web sites pretty simple. Alternately, you can learn basic *hypertext transfer markup language* (HTML) coding from this book and build Web pages with your existing word processing program, like Microsoft Notepad or Wordpad which come bundled with Windows 95 and 98.

The web authoring software packages are good, but you will find that your creativity will be curtailed by software limitations. If you understand even basic HTML coding, the possibilities of getting your Web site to look exactly as you want it to look are much greater. It is similar to the difference between using a pre-planned template to create something and creating it from scratch. Personally, I believe knowledge of basic HTML coding will make your future online business endeavors more understandable and therefore more fruitful, even if you decide to try the web authoring software later. You may even find out you enjoy creating Web sites so much that you begin offering it as a service to other local businesses.

A word of caution: the Internet is such a huge place that having a Web site, even a great looking one, doesn't mean automatic business. You have to do some things that will attract people and keep them coming back for more. One of those things is making your expertise available in the form of free information on your site. While initially you may struggle with the concept of donating your experience to the public domain, and free of charge no less, successful entrepreneurs have found it one of the keys to success. Some business owners actually post enough information about the services they offer that you could do it yourself! Their hope is that you will soon realize that you don't have the time. The fact that they are willing to share this information catches your attention and builds trust. It's an effective marketing tool, and it works!

That being said, I still recommend that if you are an individual dealer or small retailer and you decide to create a site to market your merchandise, do it more for your image, ego and personal satisfaction than for sales. As controversial as that might sound, the fact is that the great majority of small business owners who specialize in antiques, collectibles, and retail merchandise do not sell a lot from their personal or business Web sites. As more and more people flock to the online masses and begin to trust shopping in that venue that may change, but for now it is the *unique* products and services that do well. If you are selling retail merchandise available other places, antiques and collectibles, or other items that consumers can find elsewhere, you are but one of many fish residing in the Internet sea. Unless you have a fair amount of money to invest and/or time to expend in promoting your site, chances are that it will go pretty much unnoticed. Most sellers have found that the established online auctions and malls are much more lucrative.

Make sure you visit the online auctions and list some items for sale with one or more of them. Although most are not free to use, the fees charged by these sites pale in comparison to the fees charged by a conventional auction house. For instance, if you place an item for sale on eBay™ and start the bidding at under $10 with no reserve, your listing fee is a mere $.25, which is nonrefundable. When your item sells, there is a sliding commission scale of 5% of the price from $.01 to $25, and 2.5% of the amount that falls between $25.01 and $1,000. If your item sells for $50, your commission would be $1.88 and your total expenses, including the listing fee, $2.13. Send this item to your favorite auction house and you'll probably be charged $12.50, or 25%, for the same sale. The bottom line: if you're willing to do the packing and shipping (which the buyer also pays for), you can increase your net profits significantly.

Even though this is a relatively new market, online auction users are already becoming more sophisticated and the prices realized for more common antiques and collectibles don't fly into the stratosphere as they once did. However, there is still an excellent chance that you will sell items that have been sitting around in your shop or booth forever. And don't be surprised if they bring more than your original asking price.

What about buying for resale at the online auctions? Yes, it can be done. I have purchased many items online that I successfully resold from an antiques mall booth location. But the bargains are few and far between, and there is a lot of merchandise you won't be interested in that has to be sifted through to find the gems. The competition can be pretty fierce, especially during the last five minutes of the auction. It's not unusual to invest a lot of time looking, find a great piece, place a bid, sit up late at night waiting for the auction to end, and have it snatched away from you at the last second or watch it go too high to qualify for resale. Sounds like a conventional auction, doesn't it? Only you're not standing in the rain while all of this is going on.

One item of note, now that there is some history to look at, is that there is a strong case that can be made for using the "seasonal" aspects of online auctions to your advantage. Prices realized seem to follow the rules that experienced retailers already know—business for many items is off in the summer and peaks in the six weeks before Christmas. Just as a retailer sees a drop in customers and revenue when business is off, the online seller will see a drop in final bid prices for merchandise. But don't despair—if you use the online auctions to purchase for resale in other venues, it's a buying opportunity! It is even possible to buy merchandise during the summer at depressed prices and resell it using the very same auction service in December for a profit.

When I first began using the online auctions as a source of buying, it was not unusual for me to spend most of the day patrolling sites, evaluating descriptions, studying photos, e-mailing sellers with questions, and placing bids. Most of the time was spent doing the sifting—there are literally thousands of available items on some sites. If you are a collector, or a dealer that specializes in one or two types of merchandise, you can use the *search* functions made available on most sites. As a general line dealer looking for good buys over a broad range of categories, you're much more limited, so expect to spend a lot of time online.

If you're not comfortable selling in an auction environment and prefer to offer your items at a fixed price, another outlet for your merchandise is an online antique mall. Again, there are fees involved, but they are much less than the cost of maintaining a conventional shop or booth. There are several very good ones available, and you can provide a photo and description of your items.

Have you heard about electronic bulletin boards? Now we're back into the freebies, and there are lots of them around where you can post a free classified ad. Many times bulletin boards are part of an online community of people with like interests, complete with chat rooms and e-mail lists. Networking with these other collectors can be a good way to sell your items, too.

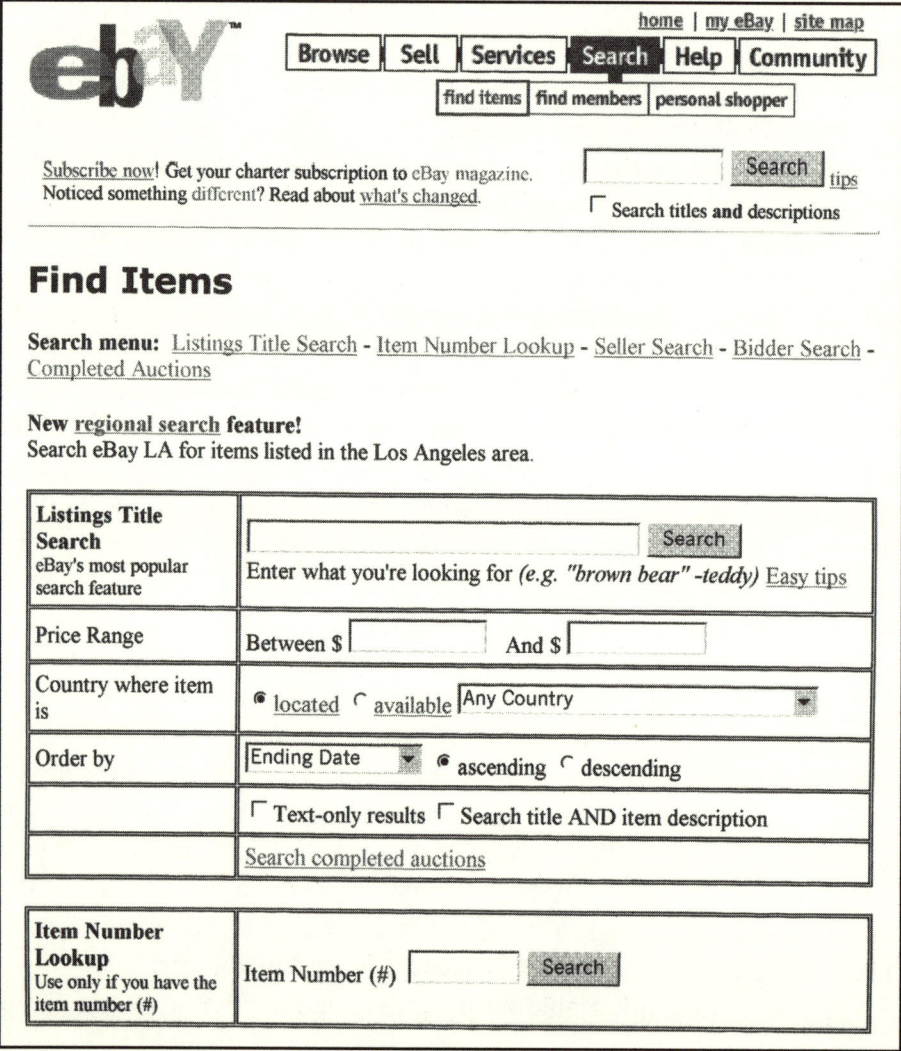

Let's not forget the intangibles like the educational materials available on the Internet. Knowledge is power, and you can become quite powerful by taking advantage of the information online. The more you know about your business, the better chance you stand of understanding a good deal when it becomes available.

I can't stress enough that all of this demands a time commitment. If you plan to make the Internet an integral part of your business, you should investigate using the fastest equipment available. Check with your local cable TV company to find out if Internet cable access is available where you live. Cable connections are much faster than a 56K-modem connection, and the price should start to decline as the service becomes available in more areas and competition for your business heats up. Right now, if you can get it, there is typically an installation charge of about $150.00 and monthly access fees approaching $50.00. It should

Seller Search Find all items currently listed by a specific seller	[_____] Search User ID or email address of seller. See your favorite seller's listings.
Include bidder emails	⦿ No ◯ Yes
Completed items too?	⦿ No ◯ All ◯ Last Day ◯ Last 2 Days ◯ Last Week ◯ Last 2 Weeks
Order by	◯ Newest first ⦿ Oldest first ◯ Auction end ◯ Current price
# of items per page	25

Bidder Search Find all items currently bid upon by a bidder	[_____] Search User ID or email address of bidder. Use if you want to see what you bid on.
Completed items too?	⦿ No ◯ Yes
Even if not high bidder?	⦿ Yes, even if not the high bidder ◯ No, only if high bidder
# of items per page	25

Completed Auctions Find auctions that have completed	[_____] Search Words to search for in title *(e.g. "brown bear" -teddy)* Easy tips
Order by	Ending Date ⦿ ascending ◯ descending
	☐ Text-only results

get you at least twice the speed of your 56K hookup, so you have to do the math and decide how much your time is worth. You can spend all of your waking hours online if you want to; I did exactly that when I first started using the Internet to buy and sell antiques and collectibles but soon found myself missing conventional auctions and buying trips out of town. And I'll let you in on a little secret: while it's a fantastic tool for low-overhead selling, your chances of finding that "great buy" are just as good, and perhaps better, in an antique mall or flea market than at an Internet auction. The quality items up for bid on the big auction sites have a mysterious way of consistently selling at prices near the top of what the market will bear. If an item doesn't get a lot of bids, the reserve price protects the seller from having to accept less than he wants. Finding the combination of an item with no reserve as well as a low bid price takes time, diligent study, and expertise on what sells in your area. But it can be done!

Always Let Your Conscience Be Your Guide

Most employers are just beginning to recognize the benefits of utilizing technology for off-site workers, and some are allowing employees to spend part of their time working at home. This action not only promotes employees being happier, in many cases some increase in productivity is observed. When you get a responsible employee away from the constant phone calls and interruptions that exist in many companies and allow them to work hours that give them some degree of schedule flexibility, positive results can be obtained. For many American workers, however, the outlook does not seem as bright as government statistics would have you believe, and the scenery never changes.

We live in an age where home entrepreneurs have an opportunity to flourish. There is nothing quite like the feeling of breaking free of the shackles that bind you when you work for someone else. While it may not be for everyone, the landscape of the American worker is changing radically as more and more people are leaving the "security" of a corporate job to try making it on their own.

The Internet has made this possible, and helping you in whatever capacity you choose to use it is what this book is about. I do not have the desire (or the right) to tell you how to use this information, and I certainly don't recommend quitting your job tomorrow. Ease into this slowly, see if it is for you, and make your own decision. I will only say that I have no regrets about leaving corporate America!

Chapter 2
The Personal Touch circa 1999

The antiques business used to be a very personal one. Dealers knew what their regular clients liked, and that helped guide them in their buying habits. Many items were purchased simply because the dealer knew he had a ready buyer for them. Customers knew they were getting the "real McCoy" because they trusted their dealer to sell them only merchandise that was, without a doubt, as old as the dealer represented it.

Dealers had to be part salesperson, because convincing someone to buy often meant knowing the history of the item and being able to impart that information to the prospective buyer in an interesting way. Relationships were built, and the frequent buyer of antiques had a favorite dealer just as they did a favorite dentist or doctor.

That started to change in the 1970s with the introduction of the antique mall. Dealers no longer had to be present to sell their merchandise, as workers hired by the mall management staffed the malls. While many of these workers were dealers themselves, there was no way they could remember what was in every booth let alone know some history of each item in the mall. The antiques business became more impersonal, and some buyers became wary of this new type of selling and stayed away. To this day I know people who will not purchase an antique from a mall booth unless they can talk to the dealer first.

Online auctions again make it possible for customers to reach dealers, not face to face, but via e-mail. As online auction buyers become more experienced, they will begin to ask more questions about merchandise listed for sale. They will again want to know the details and histories of expensive purchases before placing their bids. While some will argue that the personal touch isn't fully realized unless you are in the same room with the other person, good communication skills can be easily adapted to the e-mail environment. Many long-lasting friendships are made this way—I still correspond regularly with the person who bought the first item I ever listed online. While obviously you can't stay in touch with everyone, you will find yourself building online relationships, sharing ideas, and expanding your overall knowledge of this business. Some online acquaintances become good friends that you will finally meet face to face one day because you want to.

I believe that the Internet actually fosters this type of communication because you can't form judgments based on appearance. You get to know a person based on intangibles like how well they express themselves using e-mail, or how much knowledge they have about antiques, before you prejudge them based on what they look like. How many methods of communication are available today where the CEO's and presidents of companies still read and answer their messages? With e-mail, most still do. This can be a powerful tool when used properly, and you can learn more about the antiques business than would ever have been possible without it.

Here's an example of learning about an item you can't identify. I recently acquired a humidor marked with the Nippon green wreath mark. The humidor has, all the way around the circumference, what appear to be Chinese men in raised relief. I found it in an antique mall (actually I was steered to it by the co-owner, who seems to have a good feel for quality and knows what I like). Now, I'm no expert in Nippon, but I had enough knowledge to know that a raised relief humidor was probably desirable. Besides, the humidor "felt" like a quality piece—you dealers who have been in this business for awhile know what I mean, and I purchased it.

Upon returning home, I promptly began researching the "china humidor" in books and on the Internet. I found Nippon raised relief humidors, some selling for 10-15 times what I paid for this particular one—but found no examples with the Chinese men. Then, as I was browsing the eBay auctions that had already ended looking for examples, I noticed an eBay user had just purchased a Nippon raised relief humidor and his e-mail address had the word "Nippon" in it! Hey, why not! I contacted him and he was able to give me information on the age and current market value of the humidor. He even offered to purchase it should I ever want to part with it, and his name is now tucked away in my e-mail address book. The only reason I didn't negotiate a sale with him right away is that my wife also recognizes quality, and the humidor is now safely residing in our "favorite treasures" china cabinet. You experienced dealers know what I mean by that too.

You will find that more times than not, e-mail messages for information to strangers you have reason to believe know more than you on a subject are returned promptly and courteously. Identify yourself, explain why you think the person you are contacting might be able to help, ask for help, and thank them for their time.

In your everyday dealings online, how do you cultivate this golden opportunity? By employing good customer service skills, just as you would if you were selling from your personal antiques store. And in fact, you are, but now your store is online.

Virtual Customer Service

Let's look at some of the old standby rules of customer service and see how they apply to today's Internet selling. You will see that the old rules still apply, with one notable exception, and not abiding by them online can multiply the negative effects exponentially.

1. Customers tell twice as many people about an unsatisfactory transaction as they do about a positive one. The ramifications of this one when using online auctions cannot be underestimated. Most online auctions allow users to leave feedback about someone they have dealt with, and everyone who is registered has access to viewing it. If your feedback file contains more than 2-3 negative comments, you are putting up a red flag to prospective buyers. Put simply, if they think you aren't honest, they won't bid on your auctions. It is up to you to represent your items correctly and honestly.

2. If you resolve a complaint immediately, 95% of customers will feel satisfied. And a satisfied customer means a positive feedback entry, even if the transaction did not go exactly as they would have liked. The first response you make to an e-mail message from a dissatisfied customer is the one they will remember, so make sure they understand immediately that you are there to help them resolve the problem. If you respond in a surly, negative tone or resolve the problem only after several heated e-mail exchanges, you lose.

3. The customer is always right. At the risk of sounding cynical (my wife says I am—I prefer to label myself a realist), today we live in a world where I can't subscribe to this steadfast rule. There are too many dishonest people, and now they are able to hide behind the mask of the Internet and be dishonest incognito, which only gives them more reason to do it. Of course, you must still give people the benefit of the doubt, and you should try to avoid telling a customer they are wrong even if you know they are. Use your negotiating skills to work out something acceptable to both of you. If everything you try fails, and you're sure you are dealing with a dishonest customer, tell them (be as unthreatening as you can in case they might still come around) that you intend to report them to the Internet Fraud

Watch and the Better Business Bureau. If the item was sold using online auctions, also report them to the auction itself and leave negative feedback for them.

4. Offer your customers some "value added" services. This will earn you a reputation as a great online seller as fast as anything else you can do. For instance, eBay™ seller Brad Bonham (bbonham@mtneer.net) of Beckley, West Virginia offers his buyers a $1.00 discount for paying with a money order. According to Brad, "I myself use money orders to pay, and that is the way I prefer to be paid." As anyone who has had the misfortune of receiving a bad check knows, this is relatively cheap insurance for the seller and it doubles as a value added to the customer. That's a WIN-WIN in the business world. Brad also uses his eBay™ "About Me" page to outline his business policies, which leads me to…

1. Make sure the customer has access to your business policies. I believe this is the most important thing you can do when running an online business to avoid misunderstandings. In fact, I feel so strongly about this that I would urge the online auctions and malls to *require* sellers to list their policies, especially their return policies, as a condition of selling on their sites. eBay™ makes a page available to everyone who registers with them called simply "About Me" that can be personalized—why not have a page that requires sellers to list their terms of doing business before they are allowed to place an item up for auction or sale? That way, if you have a fair return policy, people can check that before bidding and feel more comfortable purchasing your merchandise. This can also afford you more protection from having items returned if you have a no return policy. I don't recommend a no return policy, especially for Internet selling, and in fact I encourage buyers not to bid on things they can't touch and can't return, but the choice is yours. As online buyers become more sophisticated they will be asking more questions before bidding. You may as well make the information available to them—it will save you time and trouble as you build your business.

A few of the things I do to build trust and confidence with people who buy from me using the online auctions are:

1. Not charge a handling fee unless there is extensive time or material involved in the shipping

2. Offer a choice, with rate quotes, for both parcel post or priority mail shipping for heavy items

3. Suggest, but not require, the packages be insured—I let the buyer decide if they want to spend the extra money for insurance.

Use common sense and be fair. Your positive feedback will grow, thereby establishing you as one of the best online sellers. Bidders do look at feedback numbers, if not the feedback itself, and will hesitate if you have shown to be unreliable in the past.

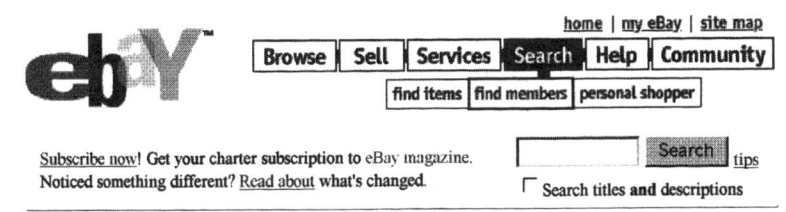

This page is maintained by bbonham@mtneer.net (80)

Welcome fellow junkers, and come on in!

Hi, my name is Brad Bonham, and not long ago I stumbled upon this place called ebay. If you are new, welcome, settle on in, and enjoy the ride. If you are a serious collector, dealer, or combination of both (such as myself), then you are going to find ebay an invaluable tool and resource. Many hours will be spent here. You crusty old timers with those triple+ numbers beside of your user ID know exactly what I'm talking about, I am sure.

My girlfriend/probably someday future wife and I both enjoy dabbling in old stuff. Both Deb and I mainly collect pottery. (With a slight emphasis on Weller) I myself sort of grew up, stubbing my toes on old stuff that my mom constantly packed into our ever-shrinking home, and at the time despised and cursed every new old piece that come through the doors. Now I find the memories of stubbing toes and cursing the old junk even more valuable then the old junk that my toes were stubbed on to begin with. Maybe that is why I eventually come to fall in love with the whole business of it all. Who knows. I do know that Deb become hooked on it in no time, and her eye for fine collectable old stuff is becoming just as attuned as mine.

If you are purchasing an item from me, please rest assured that I guarantee that item as described, and if for any reason you are not satisfied, I will refund all but shipping and ebay charge. If an unreasonable error is made on my part, then I will make a full refund as long as I am notified within 7 days receipt. I myself use money orders to pay, and that is the way I prefer to be paid. Please deduct $1.00 from your total amount if you are paying with a money order. I hold items until personal checks clear.

If I am purchasing an item from you, please rest assured that I am a prompt payer, and all payments are made with a USPS money order. I am a customer that will remember you if I am pleased with the item and service, and will try to patronize your auctions. Just check out the small amount of feedback that is starting to build up.

Chapter 3
Success Stories

How are people who use the Internet everyday to buy and sell faring? How do those dealers you see with thousands of feedback entries do it? I've interviewed some of them, and they gave me their impressions and stories about using the Internet. I share them now, both as testimonials to the effectiveness of this tool and in the hopes that you will gain some insight into successful online selling.

Jeanene and Charles Olsen
Live Oak Antiques
Hico, Texas
eBay User ID: Liveoak

"I guess what we think about eBay™ and other auctions is that we do them as we can and don't have to go to work for someone else. There's no commuting, it's fun buying stuff for resale, and we don't have to dress up. We can take breaks when we like, and no one monitors how many trips we make to the bathroom. We can yell at each other and no one will write us up, we make the money we want to (usually) and it's ours-we don't have to share. As you can see, we think there are a lot of perks.

About the sense of community-yes, there are definitely some very nice people. Some we've kept in contact with, others we haven't, but wish we had. We've become so busy it became difficult to send the personal e-mail when there were so many business e-mails to attend to. Periodically, I do send updates to some people-and have made some friends in far away countries that we'd like to visit.

Now for the things we don't like about online auctions. People sometimes pay with bad checks or don't pay at all. Occasionally people don't like the merchandise and it's our fault because they haven't read a complete description of the item. It's a lot of work listing, taking pictures, processing photos, etc.-we sometimes work 100 hours in a week taking care of online auction business during our busy season.

The online business is just like any other-both perks and drawbacks. The main thing we really like is being able to do this business from home, and it's more lucrative than being in an antique mall.

We first began using eBay in December 1997. At first we didn't even post pictures because we hadn't figured out how to use our digital camera, and then it took us awhile to learn how to FTP. I have been buying and selling antiques occasionally for nearly 30 years, and still have the first three real antiques we bought 34 years ago-a grandfather clock, ladies writing desk, and a 19th century syrup pitcher (I've collected pitchers for more than 30 years). Then 5-1/2 years ago, we started doing it full time.

At one point, we had booths in four different malls, all within a 100-mile radius of home. It took a lot of time and a lot of money investing in inventory. How I wish for those days five years ago when I could find good dishes, glassware, and other collectibles for 10 cents on the dollar!

Charles had no experience in the antiques business. He was an insurance adjuster for 27 years before he retired. He's learned a great deal going with me to auctions, malls, estate sales, garage sales, and reading all my research books. Charles has a BS in education. I have a BA in speech and an MS in communication. Both of us have also taken accounting-which we need with two home based businesses-and other business and management courses. Charles has to stay current with his adjuster's license since he still does independent adjusting work for high-risk companies.

My own career has been a patchwork of various positions, mainly because we moved so many times with Charles' company. I have been a secretary (too many times), a dental assistant, library assistant, advertising agency account specialist and copywriter, and the job I retired from was employee relations specialist with a large supermarket chain.

We have used Amazon.com, but frankly, we don't get as good response from high bidders at the end of auctions as we do with eBay. We've had a higher no pay rate than we ever had with eBay. One thing about it though, we've sold some higher dollar merchandise there than eBay. We've sold items for $100+ that wouldn't even have gotten a bid on eBay. Go figure!!!

We also tried Auction Universe, but weren't very enamored with it. It's tough keeping track of several different auctions and the different numbering systems.

Customer service is important. For example, an auction ended on 12/16/98 and we received a money order by express mail so we could send by express mail for Christmas delivery. We had the item packed and ready to go on 12/19/98, and paid over $21.00 to send it express to Seattle, Washington. When the item was not there by 12/23/98, we called the post office to trace it and were told it was being delivered that day.

We called the buyer long distance and told her what we'd learned, but received a message the next day that the package still hadn't been delivered. To make a long story short, it wasn't delivered until 12/30/99. We submitted a claim to the post office and were able to refund the buyer the price of the express mail. The buyer was really pleased that we had tried to get everything done as she'd requested. Had we just told her we had no control over the post office, she'd have been very upset with USPS and with us.

Also, in early June 1999 an international customer complained that the customs form was filled out incorrectly and it had cost them $24.00 in duty/customs fees. We responded saying that we had used the form the post office insisted on, but since we live in a rural area the postal worker may have been unfamiliar with correct procedure. We offered to refund the $24 (it was on a $175 item) because we believe in customer satisfaction. While sometimes we aren't satisfied with the way a transaction is handled, we try to give some measure of real satisfaction to our customers. The way messages are worded and the promptness of those messages goes a long way to keep customers satisfied."

Brad Bonham
Beckley, West Virginia
eBay User ID: bbonham@mtneer.net

"I prefer money orders as payment, and offer a $1.00 discount to buyers who pay that way. This policy has generated a good response-about 90% of my customers pay that way now since the discount has been offered.

I have only been doing eBay™ for about three months now, and the sales there have more than tripled what I do locally. As a buyer and pottery collector, I have had the opportunity to buy pieces daily that would normally take months or years to find. I see this thing becoming really huge in the future.

I have thought about adding to my sales policy the offer of free shipping for any item that reaches a certain amount, such as $50 or $100. I know that shipping is a consideration when purchasing online, and if someone is charging $10 for shipping on an item I know costs less than $6 to ship, I will pass that auction up.

Another thing I have considered is writing up a short paragraph for new users/bidders about sniping. I admit that I will bid on an auction, and if I am immediately outbid, I will watch the auction till the very end, and then come in at the last minute and drop in exactly what I am willing to pay. It is a way to save money on an item if the reserve is met, and really gets the adrenaline pumping, especially if someone else is doing the same. This would be a "fair warning" to bidders against me if they take the time to read about the person they are bidding against.

One thing I do before listing is plan. If I have only one item of a certain category, I will hold off until I find several more so I can link them all together in each auction. I write up all of the like auctions and save them to my hard drive, then list all at the same time. For instance, right now I have 21 window frames and 9 pieces of Roseville pottery listed. The window auctions mention that I have others and I have placed a link in there to my other auctions list-the same goes for the Roseville. This will maximize exposure at minimal costs if you feature an auction and then link it to several others that are not featured. It is like featuring all of them for the price of one.

With the window frames I also have spread them out in several different categories to get even more exposure. I listed them in the 'Antiques-Architectural,' the 'Antiques-General,' the 'Antiques-Primitives' and the 'Collectibles-Decorating General' categories. They have been on less than 20 hours and more than 1/3 of them have been bid on. I did the same thing with the Roseville. I have also done this with a collection of silver dollars that I acquired (109 in all) and every single one of them sold with about 75% of the bidders buying in multiples. The save on shipping clause seems to catch their attention!

Another thing I do is set my reserve just a little bit high. Most of this stuff is really hard to find and with eBay the way it is, 'book price' does not seem to apply anymore. There are certain pieces of Weller pottery that I personally collect, and I will pay well over book price if it is a piece that either doesn't come up very often or one I just simply have to have. I'm sure there are thousands of others out there just like me.

Although I might be a little new to the game, I am starting to feel that I have sellers bragging rights for the simple fact that in two of less than 25 auctions I've held I have made nearly $2,000 after costs. You can't do that around here very easily, even in a good month. My sales percentage is around 85%, and I hope to boost that. If everyone is doing as well as I, then there are a lot of people making a lot of money. I must admit that I am spending a lot also to support the pottery habit, and am spending most of it online."

Mike and Debbie Werle
Irving, Texas
http://rampages.onramp.net/~debbyemp
Debby's Online Auction
www.debbys.com

"The auction www.debbys.com was started in late 1996 to sell collectibles and antiques from our store, Debby's Emporium. We are on a corner, and discovered the Internet when the city tore up first one street for a year and then the other for a year. This killed our walk-in traffic. Having been at this site since 1980, we were forced to seek other markets. It was the best thing that ever happened to us. We started on eBay™ and then wanted to try one of our own.

At this time, we have small items in the $1.00 range for sale on our auction site. We also use it as support (pictures and secure credit service) for our sales on the major action sites. Anyone can list and sell whatever they wish at no charge. If we don't have a category, we can create it.

We took bids from professional web design companies and selected Mark Blythe at Creativision to create the site for us. We have no training in this area and it has been a strictly learn as you go experience. Since we had to "make a living" at the same time, we couldn't take the time to learn what we needed to know and then do it ourselves. At the time we did it, there wasn't pre-designed software that we could find that was satisfactory.

Getting on the Internet was the best thing we've ever done, because over the years we've had some incredible merchandise and have been unable to get it before the market that would appreciate it. On the web, the merchandise is there for the whole world to see.

If nothing else, the auction site web space has been worth it as a place to store all the photos of all our merchandise. We have around 100MB of space. Verisign also makes it possible for us to take credit cards on line securely. The majority of our business comes from the large, established auctions.

As far as sales are concerned, our own auction site and Web page has been a disappointment. When we set it up we thought people would flock to it and it would take right off. As I said before, we were ignorant at that time about what would be involved. To make it successful, more time than we have needs to be devoted to it. There are a lot of free things that could be done to promote it, but it all takes lots of time. As I said before, we have to make a living at the same time. The business is not a hobby with us, but our sole source of income.

We still have high hopes for it in the future. Our daughter Michelle is involved with a web development company and hopefully she'll learn enough to help us make it a success in the future.

I would tell anyone thinking of doing mail order in whatever form they choose that they really need to think it through. This is a very labor-intensive proposition. You don't just sit at your computer and list items for sale. Items must be photographed. You have to develop a system for processing the merchandise from purchase to shipment. Sold items must be packaged and shipped either by carrying them physically to the post office or UPS or readied for UPS pickup. The paperwork alone is staggering, keeping up with who bought what, whether they've paid, and getting the proper item shipped to the proper buyer. I read and process about 200 e-mails per day in addition to the ones I initiate.

I'd rather not state our volume. I will say that we aren't getting rich, but making what we consider a comfortable living. We work an average of 10 hours a day, 5 days a week. In addition, we have 6-7 part-time employees that help. When we aren't at the shop, we're usually on the lookout for merchandise. Keep in mind that we love what we do, so it really isn't as bad as it sounds. It would really be drudgery if we didn't. Our children are grown with lives of their own, so we do have the flexibility to take off when we want to."

Jon & Faith Nelson
Montoursville, PA
eBay User ID: nelsons3jf@aol.com

"We have been expanding our enterprise for over two years. Faith and I do eBay™ full time, and have a temporary employee too.

We find eBay™ a great way to keep us very busy. We always are amazed at how people think that selling on eBay™ is so easy. Actually it is much more involved than it first appears. Faith goes to auctions and buys items. She scans and puts items onto eBay™. I am involved in closing the auctions once they end, billing and packing, and the accounting. The temporary employee helps Faith 2/3 of the time with scanning and uploading pictures and 1/3 with packing. We use Quickbooks software for the invoicing, and tracking our sales.

We enjoy the work on eBay™, but it is much more involved than many people think. We have seen many dealers start selling on eBay™, only to quit after several months, because it is not easy for the unorganized.

We attempt to limit ourselves to an eight-hour day, which begins after we take our three-year-old son to preschool. We spend from 8AM to 4PM at the computer, but might spend three more hours organizing and doing paperwork, until 8PM, away from the computer. The weekends are reduced to 3-4 hours a day. We list two days a week and try for 100 new auctions on those days. All said, we probably average ten hours a day during the weekdays and four hours on weekends.

Faith is the originator of our selling on eBay. She is a button collector, so it started as a way to sell the extra buttons that she had and grew from there. We have been doing this full time for almost two years. Both of us have been into antiques for awhile.

We mostly sell paper items, postcards, trade cards, documents, prints, books, etc. We also sell consignment items for our friends who have no interest in using a computer to sell on eBay.

Faith was an Administrator at a large engineering firm in Houston, and I was in the automotive industry working for a foreign manufacturer for many years

We always try to turn around a customers eBay win within 24 hours of receiving payment, and try to respond to an eBay winner within 3 hours of the end of an auction. We will also ship to anywhere in the world. We have shipped to customers in over 36 countries representing every continent except Africa.

I find that Quickbooks is great for invoicing and tracking costs. I use it exclusively and have not used any other accounting programs. Faith does not find a need for it doing her end of the business. Our part-timer is hired through a temp agency, so all taxes are paid by them."

L & E Collectibles
eBay User ID: collectibles@sprintmail.com

"We've been doing eBay for two years now, starting in February of 1997 after a friend had been raving about it for about 6 months. I finally decided to see what it was all about-posted a few things-and was hooked! I had my own Disneyana business for about six years when I started eBay. I was doing shows and a monthly list/newsletter of things for sale. My roommate started helping me with the shipping that first summer and he quit his job by the end of the summer to help me full time! We now have a third full-time person and a part-timer nights/weekends to do the shipping-eBay is all we do! Amazing, isn't it? Who would have thought 5 years ago that this could be done!

    I buy out stores that are going out of business and store overstocks, etc., or if I see a really good deal on something then I'll buy it to resell. About a year ago I contracted with a friend who does computer work for Boeing to write me an automated program to do eBay-I was lucky to get 20 things a day up manually and now we've listed as many as 500 things in one day with our program."

Chapter 4
What's In It For Me?

In a word, everything! I won't bore you with too many details because most of us hear stories all the time about the expansion of the Internet as a shopping source. Here are a few figures to get your money-making glands salivating.

From late 1995 until early 1997, the statistics reported by America Online, CompuServe, and Prodigy would indicate that the number of individuals accessing the Internet through one of these three services jumped nearly 500%! The actual figures reported added up to over 14 million people! And this does not account for the millions more who by that time were accessing the Internet through local and national Internet Service Providers other than these three.

Numbers like this prompted some organizations to forecast that every home would be on the Internet by the early years of the new millenium. While this is highly unlikely, it is a fact that your potential audience is growing by leaps and bounds. And that audience has more purchasing power than most of us see in our shops and stores in a lifetime.

While tracking growth in this fast-paced new medium is difficult, there is no doubt that an increase in users will equal an increase in the amount of money spent online to purchase goods and services. There are varying figures as to the amount of online sales that occurred in 1997 and 1998 but even the lowest estimates are lofty numbers. If you make an assumption that revenue will increase proportionally to the increased number of users and go by the low estimates as your basis, you still arrive at a figure in the neighborhood of 3.5 billion dollars in online sales by the end of 1999. I believe that not only will the number of Internet users continue to grow, per capita spending will also increase as online shoppers become more comfortable with giving their credit card information through secure servers.

Boom!

Here's another fact to think about. How long have you been hearing about the increased significance that maturing baby boomers will have on the economy? During the Baby Boom (1946-1964), 79 million people were born, accounting for nearly one third of the population today.

During the years 1995 to 2005 America will definitely age, and the demographics are forecast to change as follows:

0 to 17 years old	+6%
18 to 34 years old	-3%
35-54 years old	+16%
55+ years old	+20%

While baby boomers are noted for their young attitudes, better health, and longevity, the fact remains that there will be a significant number of Americans spending more time at home. Many of these seniors will turn to the Internet for entertainment, information, services, and shopping. The potential is there—you must find and develop your slice of this pie before it's gone. Now is the time.

Ground Zero

How does near-zero overhead sound? If you tackle your online business on a part-time basis and do everything yourself, it is possible to incur very few expenses other than your computer, telephone line, Internet access, and this book! Should you decide to grow your business and add employees, overhead costs can still held to a minimum—a cyberspace storefront costs much less to maintain than brick and mortar. The antiques and collectibles dealers I spoke to about this topic agreed that decreased overhead was a big plus for their online operations, with some reporting profits as high as 60% online.

Reaching Out for a Song

After reading the chapter on HTML, you will have the tools and knowledge you need to create your own working Web site. Even if you decide to retain the services of a professional Web site designer, the cost for a basic site should be much less than getting color brochures printed. Speaking of printing, once your brochures are printed if you find a mistake you either live with it or throw them away. With a Web site, changes can be made inexpensively (or free if you do it yourself) in a matter of minutes. Actually it is advisable to make frequent changes to your site, and regularly offer new information to keep surfers coming back.

Do you have an existing business that invests a lot of time answering customer questions, or do you spend a lot of money on phone bills? Orders can be taken, questions answered, and information exchanged using e-mail, saving you wear and tear on your phone costs. You can create a section of your Web site that answers frequently asked questions (FAQ). Depending on the nature of your business, this action alone can cut down on customer service expenses dramatically.

24/7

How much would it cost you to keep your business open 24 hours a day, seven days a week? When you have an Internet presence, it happens automatically. Whether you create a storefront or list items for sale with an Internet auction or mall, anybody with Internet access can find you any time of the day or night. You don't even have to worry about being robbed at 2AM!

Even Steven

One of the biggest inducements for many entrepreneurs is that the Internet is many ways "levels the playing field" between large companies and small businesses. While it is true that big business can afford to have professional designers and virtually unlimited advertising funds, you can still be right there with a Web presence of your own. Look for needs created by the major players in your field and fill them. A good example is the multitude of software packages reviewed later in this book that make some of the business aspects of using the online auctions easier—enterprising individuals are capitalizing on the success of online auctions to make some extra money themselves.

CHAPTER 5
HTML-Dress for Success

Your Web site, should you decide to create and maintain one, becomes your business suit in the online world. Most of your customers will never meet you or see you in person. The first impressions they get won't come from your clothes, but from your Web site. If you decide you need one, you can spend hundreds and even thousands of dollars to have it implemented, or you can design and create it yourself. Really, you can!

Learning HTML can be fun and satisfying. Getting your own Web page or site can be a boost for your ego and make you feel proud. It is not, however, the most efficient way to make money selling. The Internet is too big a place for everybody to take time to come to your site, or even find it for that matter. Unless you also spend a good bit of money promoting, chances are your site will be visited infrequently.

However, having a well-designed Web site does give you an aura of professionalism with the people who do see it, and if you provide a link to it with your online auction listings you will generate some traffic. If you take the time to learn how to design and create your own site, do it more for these intangibles than for actual sales.

Let's take a minute to talk about good design as it applies to the Internet. Good design is not as intimidating as Madison Avenue would have you think. In fact, good design is based on keeping it simple. Using too many different type styles or too many graphics will only make your Web site look like a junkyard. Take a look at your favorite Internet auction sites. How many different type styles do you see? Not many, I'll bet.

There is another excellent reason to limit the use of graphics on your new storefront-load time. Graphics, especially those that aren't properly prepared, can take a long time to load into someone's browser window. Most Internet surfers won't give you the luxury of that time, and will speed off to another part of cyberspace rather than wait for your cumbersome page to load. One or two well-designed, well-placed graphics are much better than an armada of them.

What I am about to show you is by no means a comprehensive guide to HTML. There are plenty of books available if you decide to pursue this further. But when you're finished with this chapter, you will be ready and able to design and create a simple but effective Web site to market your wares and enhance your profitable Internet adventure.

Playing Tag

HTML is based on the use of tags, or codes. These tags control everything from size to color to placement. Entering tags is easy once you understand the rules. Just remember that 1) tags appear between angle brackets, 2) are usually used in pairs utilizing an opening and closing tag, and 3) closing tags are the same as opening tags but with a forward slash. It really is easy!

Let's start with a simple example. The tag for a paragraph is the letter "p" (it's even logical). So when you want to begin a new paragraph on your Web page, <p> would be your opening tag. Referring back to our rules we know almost all tags are used in pairs, opening and closing, so to end a paragraph </p> would be our closing tag. If you prefer to have your tags stand out from the surrounding text even more, you can use capital letters within the tags-it makes no difference.

You can use more than one tag with a block of text. If you would want your paragraph to appear in italic, your HTML would look like this...

<p><i>Your text here</i></p>

Notice how the closing tags are used in the reverse order from the opening ones. This is the preferred way to use multiple closing tags-the last opening tag to be used is the first one to be closed and so forth.

Here, then, are the basic tags you will use regularly with text, called formatting tags. There really aren't that many, and you will soon find out how simple this can be at a basic level. All except two must be terminated with the appropriate closing tag. Tags that require no closing are known as non-paired tags.

Formatting Tags

OPENING TAG	CLOSING TAG	USE
<h1>	</h1>	#1 heading (largest)
<h2>	</h2>	#2 heading
<h3>	</h3>	#3 heading
<h4>	</h4>	#4 heading
<h5>	</h5>	#5 heading
<h6>	</h6>	#6 heading (smallest)
<p>	</p>	Paragraph
<center>	</center>	Center
<b>	</b>	Bold
<i>	</i>	Italic
<u>	</u>	Underline
<big>	</big>	One size larger than default
<small>	</small>	One size smaller than default
 		Line break
<hr>		Horizontal Rule

Before you can display your work on your browser, you have to learn a few more tags that open and close every document, called structure tags. They don't affect the content of your page, but allow the Internet to identify your page as an HTML document and provide a title for it that is displayed by the browser. You should always use these four structure tags, if for no other reason than the adopted HTML specifications say they must be used. Structure tags also have opening and closing versions, but the <html> and <body> tags are not closed until the end of the document.

Structure Tags

OPENING TAG	CLOSING TAG	USE
<html>	</html>	Identifies document language
<head>	</head>	Identifies document type
<title>	</title>	Identifies document title
<body>	</body>	Identifies document content

Now let's apply all of this to practical use. Here's an example to show you where the tags are placed. In the case of structure tags, this placement will be used in ALL documents you create.

Our example will be a Web page for an antiques business. Note that you can use extra word spaces and the enter key at any time to make your document cosmetically easy to follow-it makes no difference in the way the page displays on the Internet. We will be doing several exercises so you may want to create a new folder on your hard drive called Exercises.

HTML Exercise 1

\<html\>
\<head\>\<title\>ABC Antiques and Collectibles Home Page\</title\>\</head\>
\<body\>
\<center\>\<h1\>ABC Antiques and Collectibles\</h1\>\</center\>
\<p\>Welcome to the home of ABC Antiques and Collectibles! We specialize in high-quality jewelry items from the Victorian era. Feel free to browse our site and contact us with any questions you might have.\</p\>
\<p\>All are of our items are guaranteed authentic. You have 30 days from the date of purchase to contact us with concerns you have about the age or condition of any piece you purchase from ABC Antiques and Collectibles.\</p\>
\</body\>
\</html\>

Believe it or not, that's all there is to creating a simple Web page. If you don't believe me, launch Notepad on your computer (you should be able to find it on a Windows 95/98 computer by clicking Start-Programs-Accessories-Notepad) and input HTML Exercise 1 just as you see it here. Save it to your Exercises folder as exer1.html (note: HTML documents must always end with the .html extension). Now launch your Web browser and, under the File menu, select Open. Type the filename and location in, or browse until you find exer1.html. When you click Open or OK you will see the fruits of your labor in your browser window, just as it would display on the Internet!

Adding Graphics

If you've used photos of your items with online auctions, you probably already know that there are two types of graphic formats the Internet supports-.JPG (JPEG format) and .GIF (GIF format). The best use of these two formats is to save photographs as .JPG files and drawings or line art as .GIF files. This will give you both the crispest reproduction of your graphic online, as well as achieve the best compression and therefore the smallest graphics files. Remember-the smaller the file, the faster it will load, and the faster it loads, the better.

Where do you find graphics to use on your Web page? If you're artistically inclined, you can draw and create your own on paper and scan them in (provided you have a scanner, of course). Or photograph your drawing with a digital camera and transfer the resulting file to your computer, although the quality may not be what you'd like. But in the absence of artistic ability, which covers most of us, you can also download images that already exist on the Internet.

Copyright laws exist for images on the Internet just as they do for photos that appear in magazines, books, newspapers, etc. If you're not sure whether or not an image is copyrighted, don't use it. But there are also plenty of sites that offer free graphics for unrestricted use. If you find something you like on these sites, you can download it from the Internet right onto your hard drive with very little trouble.

One way to see what's out there is to go to *http://www.altavista.com* and run a search for clip art. Don't forget to enclose the words clip art in quotes ("clip art")-this will narrow your results to sites where the words appear just as you typed them instead of sites where the words clip and art appear by themselves separately. You should get thousands of search results back where you can visit and explore. If you can't find a graphic or two you like by using this method, we need to talk!

For our exercise, point your browser to http://www.hobbyhouse.com and move your mouse until the cursor is pointing at the graphic of my companion book, The ABCs of Collecting Online. Right-click the mouse and a drop-down menu will appear. Select "Save this Image As" and save the file to your Exercises folder. The file will already have a name-you can use that same name or call it something else that will make it easier for you to remember. Let's call this one graphic1.jpg. That's it! The graphic is now yours to use.

Now we have to get the new graphic on your Web page. This is accomplished by using a tag, <img> (for image). <img> is a non-paired tag, so there's no closing tag used with it. However, you do have to specify the filename of the graphic (use src= to do this-src stands for source), and the filename should always be enclosed in quotes to keep it separated from the actual code. This is called adding an attribute to the tag.

To work properly, the graphic and the HTML file that uses it must be in the same folder. Here is the tag we will be adding to your HTML document:

<img src="graphic1.jpg">

Open your exer1.html file with your word processing software and, under the file menu, select Save As. Enter exer2.html in the "File Name" box and click save. You now have a duplicate of your exer1.html file that is named exer2.html. Enter the <img> tag line as you see it above between the two paragraphs of text. This will place the graphic at that location-between your two paragraphs. Now your HTML file will look like this...

Exercise 2

<html>
<head><title>ABC Antiques and Collectibles Home Page</title></head>
<body>
<center><h1>ABC Antiques and Collectibles</h1></center>
<p>Welcome to the home of ABC Antiques and Collectibles! We specialize in high-quality jewelry items from the Victorian era. Feel free to browse our site and contact us with any questions you might have.</p>
<img src="graphic1.jpg">
<p>All are of our items are guaranteed authentic. You have 30 days from the date of purchase to contact us with concerns you have about the age or condition of any piece you purchase from ABC Antiques and Collectibles.</p>
</body>
</html>

Be sure to save the file after you make the change or you will end up seeing the original version when you view it with your browser software. Open it up in your browser window. You should have a graphic displaying with your file. If it isn't, first click your Refresh button and see if it loads correctly. If the graphic is still not there, check the line you typed in with the <img> code-it must match exactly what you see in the exercise. Also make sure the graphic and the HTML file are saved in the same folder. Now, pat yourself on the back for being a successful Webmaster!

Let's learn about some more attributes you can apply to the <img> tag. Notice that when you dropped the graphic in between the two paragraphs, you have a lot of unused space beside the graphic. You can make the second paragraph wrap around the graphic by applying an align attribute. Edit your <img> line to look like this:

<img src="graphic1.jpg" align=left>

Save your file and open the HTML file in your browser window again. See how the text now wraps around the image?
Now change the attribute to align=right instead of align=left. Save and open the HTML file. You're getting pretty good at this, I'd say!
Here are the basic attributes you can use with the <img> tag. Experiment with them and you'll soon understand how easy it is to create great looking Web pages.

IMAGE ATTRIBUTES

ATTRIBUTE	USE
align=left	graphic aligns left, text wraps
align=right	graphic aligns right, text wraps
align=top	text aligns top, wrap unaffected
align=middle	text aligns middle, wrap unaffected
align=bottom	text aligns bottom, wrap unaffected
hspace=x	adds horizontal space between graphic and text-x specifies amount of pixels
vspace=x	adds vertical space between graphic and text-x specifies amount of pixels
height=x	controls height of graphic in pixels
width=x	controls width of graphic in pixels

Linking

Now we're ready to learn how to link text and/or graphics from one document to another document or graphic. For instance, earlier I recommended that you mention your Web site in the description of your online auction listings. You can build a link so that all the person reading your listing has to do is click on it to be whisked to your Web site. Again, it's done with tags, and this particular tag is called an anchor tag.

First, we need to create another document for you to link to, page two of your exercise. You create it using the same structure tags as we used in Exercises 1 and 2. Type the exercise as you see it below and save it in your Exercise folder as exer3.html.

Exercise 3

```
<html>
<head><title>ABC Antiques and Collectibles Tips Page</title></head>
<body>
<center><h1>ABC Antiques and Collectibles</h1>
<h3>Following are some tips for buying through the online auctions to protect yourself from fraud. Reprinted with permission from <i>The ABCs of Collecting Online</i> by Ray Boileau</h3></center>
<ol>
<li>Read the description twice
<li>E-mail sellers with questions
<li>Know the seller's return policy
<li>Insure your purchases
</ol>
</body>
</html>
```

Did you notice the new tag we used? <ol> is the tag for ordered list, which is a numbered list (if you prefer an unordered list, better known as a bulleted list, substitute <ul> for <ol>). After the <ol> tag, each <li> tag specifies a new line, and the list is closed with the </ol> tag. You will see the results in a minute.

Now, open up your exer2.html file and add the following text immediately after the line you used to drop the graphic in. We will be using the anchor tag I mentioned previously. Start the line with <p> followed by <a href= which is an attribute telling the anchor where to jump when

clicked. Close the anchor with </a> after the word Click, and that word becomes the hyperlink.

<p><a href="exer3.html">Click</a> here for online auction tips!!!</p>

Note that you can use other formatting tags with the anchor tag, for instance we could have used <h3> instead of <p>. Also, more than one word can be designated as the hyperlink.

OK, let's see how you did. Open exer2.html in your browser window and look at your new line below the graphic (remember, browsers are notorious for displaying an older version of a file tucked away in memory-if it doesn't look right the first thing you should do is hit Refresh). The word Click should be underlined and a different color, designating it as a hyperlink. When you click on it, you should end up being whisked to exer3.html. How do you like your numbered list?

You can also anchor a graphic so that when the graphic is clicked the jump occurs. Anchor your graphic in this way...

<a href="exer3.html"><img src="graphic1.jpg"></a>

Getting Colorful

The use of color is attention getting, no doubt about it. But color, like other elements, can be overused. Having worked in the pre-press and printing industry as a "color expert" for many years I can tell you that color is highly subjective-I would often stare in disbelief as art directors picked apart color separations or designs that I thought surely were the finest examples possible. Use color, but use it sparingly and tastefully.

Adding a color background to your Web page is a snap, and a great way to change the overall look of your page with one easy tag. Let's return to our exer2.html file, which already looks pretty good, right? Now, add this attribute to the <body> tag:

bgcolor=skyblue

The <body> tag in exer2.html should now look like this:

<body bgcolor=skyblue>

Open the file again and take a look. You've created instant background color without a lot of effort. Did you ever think it would be this easy?

Adding color to type is just as easy. Let's go to exer2.html and add another tag and attribute to create something else again. After the <h1> tag add a <font> tag with the color attribute darkblue. <font> is a paired tag, so we also need to add </font> before the </h1> tag. The <h1> line of your file should now look like this:

<h1><font color=darkblue>ABC Antiques and Collectibles</font></h1></center>

The font tag can be applied to any text headings, and even to paragraphs. Again, let me caution you not to get too creative with your newfound knowledge-too much color can quickly turn a pleasing Web page into an ugly duckling. Try to have a theme in mind when adding color, using it to tie things together rather than make them stand out.

The following chart lists a large selection of colors available for use with the <font> tag. Some, such as plum, may fit in both the red and blue families depending on your "eye", as it has nearly equal properties of both. Believe it or not these aren't the only selections available, but it's extensive enough to do your designing. Don't be surprised if not every color works with your particular browser-they don't all support each and every color. I tested every one of these with an Internet Explorer 5 browser and only a handful of them did not yield the results I expected-the ones that did not are in italic and might also give you similar results if you're using IE.

If you'd like to see how these colors (and a few others) display in your browser window against both a white and black background, visit and bookmark http://www2.4dcomm.com/livingsj/colorchart.html for a good reference page.

Red Family	firebrick	lightpink
crimson	hotpink	lightsalmon
darkorange	indianred	magenta
darkorchid	lavender	maroon
darksalmon	lavenderblush	mistyrose
deep pink	lightcoral	neonpink

orange
orangered
orchid
papayawhip
peachpuff
pink
red
salmon
scarlet
tomato
violet

Green Family
aquamarine
darkgreen
darkkhaki
darkolivegreen
darkseagreen
forestgreen
green
greenyellow
honeydew
khaki
lawngreen
lightgreen
lightseagreen
limegreen
mediumaquamarine
mediumseagreen
mediumspringgreen
mintcream
palegreen
seagreen
springgreen
yellowgreen

Blue Family
aliceblue

aqua
azure
blue
blueviolet
cornflowerblue
cyan
darkturquoise
deepskyblue
dodgerblue
lightblue
lightcyan
lightskyblue
lightsteelblue
mediumblue
mediumturquoise
midnightblue
navyblue
paleturquoise
plum
powderblue
richblue
skyblue
steelblue
turquoise

Yellow/Brown Family
beige
bisque
blanchedalmond
brown
burlywood
chocolate
cornsilk
darkgoldenrod
feldspar
goldenrod
lightyellow

linen
moccasin
oldlace
palegoldenrod
peru
rosybrown
sandybrown
sienna
tan
wheat
yellow

Metallics
brightgold
bronze
coolcopper
darkgreencopper
gold
oldgold
silver

Neutrals
antiquewhite
black
floralwhite
ghostwhite
gray
ivory
seashell
white
whitesmoke

Set the Table

Tabular material on an Internet page comes in handy for specific uses, but like color, I don't recommend using too much. You should ask yourself some questions before deciding to build a table and think about if this is really the best way to present your information. Here are some situations when tabular material is warranted:

1. You can't get the placement of a graphic where you want it in relation to surrounding text without establishing columns.
2. You have a particularly long list of information to display, such as your inventory, with prices, that you are selling online. Tables are great here, but try to keep the length of your list to a minimum, preferably so that it displays on one screen. Build several tables instead of one long one, with one for your glassware, one for your 1950s Memorabilia, etc.
3. You want to make sure your Web page visitors have an easy way to find certain information. Tables can make facts lost in paragraph form stand out better.

With that in mind, let's start with a simple table. The basic HTML codes you will use in forming any and all tables are...
<table></table> which lets your browser know where your table is starting and ending
<tr></tr> to define a table row and the end of a table row
<td></td> to define data within a column

Let's go back to our exer3.html file and insert the following HTML coding immediately after the </ol> code. Keep in mind your table, and in fact all active coding, must be placed before the </body> code.

<table>
<tr><td>001</td><td>Oak Kitchen Clock</td><td>$245.00</td></tr>

Let's evaluate what you just did. <table> simply instructs your browser that you are starting a table, therefore enabling it to understand the <tr> and <td> codes. <tr> defines the first row of your table, and <td> defines the first column of that first row. The number "001" will actually display in your browser, and the </td><td> tells your browser to end one column and start another. The words "Oak Kitchen Clock" will display, </td> ends column two, <td> begins column three. The price "$245.00" displays, </td> ends column three, and </tr> ends the first row of the table.

Now move on to the next row of your table:

<tr><td>002</td><td>Art Glass Vase</td><td>$300.00</td></tr>

And the next:

<tr><td>003</td><td>Dragnet Game</td><td>$40.00</td></tr>

End your table with </table>. Your HTML table code, which appears between the </ol> and </body> tags of your exer2.html file, should look like this:

<table>
<tr><td>001</td><td>Oak Kitchen Clock</td><td>$245.00</td></tr>
<tr><td>002</td><td>Art Glass Vase</td><td>$300.00</td></tr>
<tr><td>003</td><td>Dragnet Game</td><td>$40.00</td></tr>
</table>

Save the exer3.html file to make sure the changes are accepted, and display the updated file in your browser window. You've created a table! But it's a bit cramped, isn't it? Next we learn about some table attributes to add space to your rows and columns.

The first two attributes I want you to learn about are cellpadding and cellspacing. Both are used to open up the space within your table. The difference is that cellpadding adds space above and below the text, and cellspacing adds space between columns. Another way to say it is that cellpadding adds horizontal space and cellspacing vertical space. A value is added to each attribute in the form of an equals sign and a number. Changing the number will vary the amount of space being added.

Both of these attributes are added to the <table> code itself—remember that attributes help to further define a primary code. Add these attributes so that your <table> code now looks like this:

<table cellpadding=2 cellspacing=4>

You may want to add them one at a time and view the page each time to get a better impression of what each one does. And feel free to experiment using different number values. The table is now more open and looking better all the time!

In certain situations, a nice finishing touch is adding a border to your table. This is done with yet another attribute, aptly named border. The border attribute also uses a value, with different numbers varying the thickness of the border.

Modify your <table> code so that it now looks like this:

<table cellpadding=2 cellspacing=4 border=3>

Check out your work by viewing the updated file in your browser window. That cramped table is looking pretty professional now!

Another handy attribute is width. Width gives you the ability to stretch your table across more or less of the page without having to break lines or figure vertical space. You specify a percentage with the width attribute, and the percentage you use equals the amount of the browser window your table will fill.

Modify your <table> code again so it now looks like this:

<table cellpadding=2 cellspacing=4 border=3 width=80%>

Now display the table in your browser window, and it should stretch across 80% of the screen. This is a very useful design function, and saves you the guesswork of changing other values to achieve the same end result.

Those of you who have dabbled in HTML before might be used to seeing and using quotes around values. This was a common practice as the language was being developed, and assisted in the browser not interpreting a value as text. My experience has shown that in most cases the quotes are no longer necessary, and unless you are using an older version of Internet Explorer, Netscape, or other browser, I'd recommend you save yourself some time and effort by not using them anymore. If something doesn't display the way you expect, then put them in and see if it makes a difference.

Head of the Table

Table headers are just as easy to accomplish, and are done by using <th> and </th> codes. Table headers don't have to be used—your table might be just fine without them. But let's add some to our example to see how it works.

Add a new table row to the beginning of your table by placing a <tr> code in front of the already existing <tr> code that now defines the first table row. Next, finish the new table row by typing exactly what you see here:

<th>Item</th><th>Description</th><th>Price</th></tr>

Save your file and display in your browser window. See how easy it is! Now check this out—we will straddle a head over more than one column by using an attribute that works with the <th> code called *colspan*. Colspan uses a value to indicate the number of columns to straddle. Here's how it would work if we wanted to combine the Description and Price headings into one head that spanned two columns. Replace the line you just typed to create the table heads with this line:

<th>Item</th><th colspan=2>Description/Price</th></tr>

Are you still with me? If not, take a break and go back through it again—it's really not difficult once you get the hang of it. If you've comprehended it all the first time through, I predict you'll soon be buying some HTML books to broaden your knowledge.

Special Characters

What about those copyright and British pound symbols? Special characters are achieved by using a "code" that starts with an ampersand and a pound sign (&#) followed by a number and semicolon. When your browser sees &# it knows to look for a number following it and interpret it as a special character. For instance, return once again (we're getting a lot of mileage out of this one example, aren't we?) to *exer3.html* and type © before the word Dragnet in column three of your table. Check your work in your browser window—you should see the copyright symbol. Now let's add the date 1955 to the copyright. The table entry will now look like this:

©1955 Dragnet Game

Check it in the browser window—you've done it again! And since you know how to use them, here's a list that should cover most of the special characters you might need in your Web site building.

"	" - Quotation mark
#	# - Pound, or number sign
%	% - Percent sign
¡	¡ - Inverted exclamation
¢	¢ - Cent sign
£	£ - Pound sterling
¤	¤ - General currency sign
¥	¥ - Yen sign
¦	¦ - Broken vertical bar
§	§ - Section sign
¨	¨ - Umlaut (dieresis)
©	© - Copyright
ª	ª - Feminine ordinal
«	« - Left angle quote
¬	¬ - Not sign
-	­ - Soft hyphen
®	® - Registered trademark
¯	¯ - Macron accent
°	° - Degree sign
±	± - Plus or minus
²	² - Superscript two
³	³ - Superscript three
´	´ - Acute accent
µ	µ - Micro sign
¶	¶ - Paragraph sign
·	· - Middle dot
¸	¸ - Cedilla
¹	¹ - Superscript one
º	º - Masculine ordinal
»	» - Right angle quote

¼	&#188;	- Fraction one-fourth
½	&#189;	- Fraction one-half
¾	&#190;	- Fraction three-fourths
¿	&#191;	- Inverted question mark
À	&#192;	- Capital A, grave accent
Á	&#193;	- Capital A, acute accent
Â	&#194;	- Capital A, circumflex accent
Ã	&#195;	- Capital A, tilde
Ä	&#196;	- Capital A, dieresis or umlaut mark
Å	&#197;	- Capital A, ring
Æ	&#198;	- Capital AE dipthong (ligature)
Ç	&#199;	- Capital C, cedilla
È	&#200;	- Capital E, grave accent
É	&#201;	- Capital E, acute accent
Ê	&#202;	- Capital E, circumflex accent
Ë	&#203;	- Capital E, dieresis or umlaut mark
Ì	&#204;	- Capital I, grave accent
Í	&#205;	- Capital I, acute accent
Î	&#206;	- Capital I, circumflex accent
Ï	&#207;	- Capital I, dieresis or umlaut mark
Ð	&#208;	- Capital Eth, Icelandic
Ñ	&#209;	- Capital N, tilde
Ò	&#210;	- Capital O, grave accent
Ó	&#211;	- Capital O, acute accent
Ô	&#212;	- Capital O, circumflex accent
Õ	&#213;	- Capital O, tilde
Ö	&#214;	- Capital O, dieresis or umlaut mark
×	&#215;	- Multiply sign
Ø	&#216;	- Capital O, slash
Ù	&#217;	- Capital U, grave accent
Ú	&#218;	- Capital U, acute accent
Û	&#219;	- Capital U, circumflex accent
Ü	&#220;	- Capital U, dieresis or umlaut mark
Ý	&#221;	- Capital Y, acute accent
Þ	&#222;	- Capital THORN, Icelandic
ß	&#223;	- Small sharp s, German (sz ligature)
à	&#224;	- Small a, grave accent
á	&#225;	- Small a, acute accent
â	&#226;	- Small a, circumflex accent

ã	&#227;	- Small a, tilde
ä	&#228;	- Small a, dieresis or umlaut mark
å	&#229;	- Small a, ring
æ	&#230;	- Small ae dipthong (ligature)
ç	&#231;	- Small c, cedilla
è	&#232;	- Small e, grave accent
é	&#233;	- Small e, acute accent
ê	&#234;	- Small e, circumflex accent
ë	&#235;	- Small e, dieresis or umlaut mark
ì	&#236;	- Small i, grave accent
í	&#237;	- Small i, acute accent
î	&#238;	- Small i, circumflex accent
ï	&#239;	- Small i, dieresis or umlaut mark
ð	&#240;	- Small eth, Icelandic
ñ	&#241;	- Small n, tilde
ò	&#242;	- Small o, grave accent
ó	&#243;	- Small o, acute accent
ô	&#244;	- Small o, circumflex accent
õ	&#245;	- Small o, tilde
ö	&#246;	- Small o, dieresis or umlaut mark
÷	&#247;	- Division sign
ø	&#248;	- Small o, slash
ù	&#249;	- Small u, grave accent
ú	&#250;	- Small u, acute accent
û	&#251;	- Small u, circumflex accent
ü	&#252;	- Small u, dieresis or umlaut mark
ý	&#253;	- Small y, acute accent
þ	&#254;	- Small thorn, Icelandic
ÿ	&#255;	- Small y, dieresis or umlaut mark

Going Public

Your site looks the way you want it to look. You've tested the links and they all connect to the pages you want them to connect to. How do you take your content and make it a site that the public can access? The same way you make a photo accessible—by uploading your pages to a server! The only real difference is that your pages will have .html instead of .jpg or .gif as file name extensions. Once you upload your pages, you can access them by typing the URL into your browser window, just as you would to check a photo.

Once your Web site is uploaded to your ISP's server, test the links again to make sure they all work. If any of the links come up with an error that the page is not available, the probable cause is that the file you are trying to link to is not residing in the same folder as the file you are linking from. Either move the files that link together into the same folder, or open the HTML files and use complete URL's for all of the links, instead of just the file names.

If you decide to go all out and register a domain name (like www.johnsmith.com) you can do so by visiting the Network Solutions Web site at *http://www.networksolutions.com*. There you can access their database to see if the name you want is already taken, and to register if it isn't. You will need to know your ISP's primary and secondary server host name and IP address information to register. The cost is $70.00 for the first two years (does not include your ISP's monthly charge) or $119.00 if you just want to reserve the domain name for later use.

There are many other companies that will register your domain name for you, but they are all third parties, or "middle men" if you will. By processing your domain name through anyone else, you will pay for their services as well as the normal charge from Network Solutions, as they will end up going through Network Solutions anyway to complete the registration. While the process can be somewhat confusing, why not go directly to the source, do it yourself, and save some money! Many ISPs will register your site for free if they are going to host it, saving you some work.

Accepting Credit Cards

OK, now we're getting serious about our Web site, and our online auction sales! The next big step is to be able to accept major credit cards. By doing so, you make it possible for your customers to take advantage of good old American capitalism—buying something they can't afford. The purchase power of plastic, and the potential benefits to your business, should not be underestimated. While many have determined the cost to be prohibitive, if you're livelihood depends on your sales you should seriously consider it!

Make no mistake—accepting credit cards will boost your Web store business greatly. Some studies show that by not accepting plastic, you are losing roughly 60% of your possible business. Let's face it—Web shoppers are impatient, and want something NOW! By offering credit card sales, you are providing a service that will allow them to do just that.

Accepting credit cards will be beneficial for your online auction sales, too. You can mention in your descriptions that you accept major credit cards, and when you notify the high bidder at the end of the auction, one of their options can be to visit your Web site (increased traffic!) and use your secure server to pay by credit card.

There are two ways to safely accept credit cards over the Internet, *Secure Sockets Layer (SSL)* and *Secure Electronic Transaction (SET)*. SSL provides privacy protection by encrypting the channel between the consumer and the merchant. Because the data sent over the channel is secure, SSL is sufficient security in situations where you know and trust the merchant you are dealing with.

You can be sure your transaction is secured by SSL by looking for an unbroken key or closed lock symbol in the frame of your browser window. In addition, the merchant's URL will change from *http* to *https* when processing secure transactions.

SET allows online consumers and merchants to authenticate each other by exchanging digital certificates, or electronic identifications, before proceeding with an online transaction. This helps merchants ensure that a cardholder is legitimate and that the transaction is secure. A further benefit of SET is that it eliminates chargebacks to merchants for customer disputes when the cardholder has provided a valid SET certificate in the transaction.

Both Visa and Mastercard are committed to promoting SET, although at this time SSL is more available and, in fact, a built-in part of every Internet Explorer and Netscape browser. The best way to begin is to contact your bank or credit card processor, and ask them for help in learning more about e-commerce solutions for your business. They may direct you to a professional services company that specializes in e-commerce—this is still a new enough field that you should seek professional direction. Setting up an e-commerce account is not like learning HTML—you'll need help.

If you decide the cost of e-commerce limits you to accepting only one type of credit card, you should know that Visa has more cards worldwide than Mastercard, Discover, and American Express combined. Just in case you hit a dead end with your bank, following is a list of Visa ePay banks...

Bank One Corporation
Robert S. DalSanto
(217) 525-9793

Bank of Hawaii
Karl Watada
(808) 537-8387

Branch Bank & Trust Company
Rachel Floars
(919) 246-2302

Chase Manhattan Bank
Steve Bernstein
(718) 242-8137

Citibank
Dick Salvio
(516) 454-5446

Columbus Bank & Trust
Deby Jay
(706) 644-3323

Commerce Bank
Bruce Bienhoff
(816) 234-2735

Corestates Bank
Kristin Anderson
(215) 973-8802
Joyce Warren
(215) 973-3065

First Chicago /NBD Bank
Mike Dolsen
(313) 225-3654

First National Bank of Decatur
Mike King
(217) 425-8395

FNB Omaha
Jeff Moran
(402) 341-0500

First of America
Laurel Davis
(630) 954-3135

First Tennessee
Taylor Vaughn
(901) 523-4600

First Union
Michael Daley
(704) 374-4944

Mellon Bank
Jan Pottmeyer
(412) 234-2489

Nations Bank
Kally Kowalski
(704) 386-6010
Charmaine Cook
(704) 386-7813

Norwest Bank
Ron Ruppert
(612) 667-3741

Old Kent Financial Corporation
Harold J. Roundhouse
(616) 771-1128

Summit Bank
George Nichols
(732) 438-7247

UMB Bank
Pat Engelage
(816) 860-7045

Zions Bank
Gary Facer
(801) 524-2213
Phone (800) 255-8425

In addition, here are the preferred acquirers as supplied by Mastercard...

Chase Merchant Services
1401 NW 136th Avenue
Sunrise, FL 33323
Phone: (800) 622-2626 extension 1-4911

Comerica Merchant Alliance
P.O. Box 75000
Detroit, MI 48275-2430
Phone (810) 370-7162

Harris Bankcard Center
700 East Lake Cook Road
Buffalo Grove, IL 60089
Phone (847) 520-6405
Contact: Charlie Soria

KeyCorp
Merchant Services Customer Service Dept.
55 Public Squire, 7th Floor
Cleveland, OH 44113
Phone (800) 255-8425

Mellon Network Services
Phone (800) 343-7064
Contact: RJ Placone

Michigan National Bank
6105 West St. Joseph
Lansing, MI 48917
Phone (517) 323-6016
Contact: Sally Mohon

Midwest Payment Systems
Phone (513) 579-6145
Contact: Thomas A. Debord, VP

Norwest Card Services
7000 Vista Drive
West Des Moines, IA 50266
Phone: (515) 222-8163
Contact: Randy Remington

Wells Fargo Bank
Merchant Card Services
1200 Montego Way
Walnut Creek CA 94598
Contact: Debra Carraway
Phone: (510) 746-4069

Free Lessons for Self-Starters

You can continue your HTML education by purchasing books if you desire to go further—there are many of them available and most are good. Just be sure you browse the book (or it's description if you're buying online) to make sure you don't get one for advanced users if you're a beginner. The books are written for different experience levels, and you'll get lost quickly in an advanced one if you're new to this.

There is also some great HTML information available online free of charge. Try exploring *http://www.pongo.com* and see if you don't learn something useful! There are tutorials and help, with some geared specifically to eBay™, and a message board if you can't find what you're looking for. Overall, an excellent resource!

Before you spend your hard won money on too many books, here's another method of teaching yourself HTML. The coding that is used to build every page that you view on the World Wide Web is available for you to study, and even to save on your computer! That's right—every page ever built is available for you to learn the tricks of the trade from. If you're using Internet Explorer (Netscape offers this feature as well) as your browser, just go to the View menu and click on Source. A window will open with the HTML code of the page you are viewing right there! You can then save it and store it on your computer for future reference, or print it out and begin to compile your own notebook of Web page examples. Don't you just love the Internet!

CHAPTER 6
Being Seen in All the Right Places

Now that you have a Web site you're happy with, how can you increase the traffic coming to it? There are numerous things you can do, and should do, before or shortly after your site is posted publicly. Site exposure is mostly up to you, and the success of your Web store depends on it.

Search Engines

Now hear this! If you expect successful results from your Web site, you have to be listed by the major search engines. Many of these search engines allow you to submit site information yourself, but there are also other important things you should do to improve your chances of being seen.

Several informal studies have shown that when the average Internet user runs a search for specific keywords, if you are not among the top 20-30 listings that are returned your chances of getting frequent visitors are slim. There are keywords and tags that should be included in your HTML file to help identify you to the search engines, and selecting the proper words in the proper locations can also improve your overall ranking.

The total number of search engine sites on the Internet is approaching 2000, but it is not necessary to be registered with each and every one of them. In fact, research has shown that 80% of the searches recorded by all of the search engines are performed on just eight of the major ones. The search engines you want to make sure know about your site are Yahoo!, Excite, Altavista, Infoseek, Lycos, Hotbot, Web Crawler, and Northern Light. The good news is that you can add your site to six of these search engines at the same time **free of charge** by visiting *http://www.searchengineguide.org/addurl.htm*.

What about the Yahoo! search engine? Yahoo! is, after all, the most frequently used *portal* on the Internet. Registering your site with Yahoo! is a bit more complex than others, and therefore not easily packaged for submission with other sites. But you can register with Yahoo! too—find out how by visiting *http://docs.yahoo.com/info/suggest/*.

That leaves us with only Northern Light of the original eight search engines we discussed. Add your Web site to the Northern Light search engine at *http://www.northernlight.com/docs/regurl_help.html*. Of course, you can also visit other search engines and add your site yourself, or you can find a service that will submit your site to hundreds or thousands of search engines for a fee. For most people running a small business on the Internet, covering these eight top-notch search engines will suffice. Many of the other engines will eventually find your site anyway through the use of *spiders* and *robots,* which are programs that roam the Internet looking for Web sites to catalog.

More HTML—META Tags

The most important tag you can use in your HTML file has absolutely no bearing on the look of your Web site! This tag instead identifies the content of your site for visiting spiders and robots sent to index your site by the Internet search engines. The spiders and robots look at the information described by the <title> tag, as well as the first 100-150 characters in your first paragraph (including punctuation). This information is indexed and stored by the search engine as a description of your site.

Not surprisingly, these descriptions can be vague and sometimes meaningless as far as the actual site content is concerned. If you don't use the right words at the very outset of your Web page, the search engines don't know the difference and index your site by the words you do use. If you sell antiques and collectibles, but don't use the words "antique" or "collectible" in the first paragraph of your Web site, chances are nobody using them as keywords will find your site.

Fortunately you have an alternative method of teaching the spiders and robots what your site is really about—META tags. META tags are used in the head of your HTML file, usually right before the <title> tag, or right after the </title> tag but definitely within the parameters of the <head> and </head> tags. META tags can be assigned attributes, and we will talk about two of them here—the "keywords" attribute and the "description" attribute. Following a brief overview, we will resurrect our Exercise 2 from Chapter 5—HTML and add META tags so you're sure about the placement of them.

The "keywords" attribute is used to identify the words you want the search engine to index and store—words to be recognized by the search engine when someone runs a search. In other words, if someone visiting the Altavista search engine searches for the word "antique", if you have identified the word "antique" in your META tag your site is one of the listings the search engine should return. It will, of course, also return listings for many other sites that have used this same keyword, but to not appear in the list at all is much worse.

The "description" attribute simply instructs the search engine as to the exact words you want used as the title of your Web site in their listings. Avoid identifying your site as "the best site on the Internet" or other similar statement, as this is considered an amateur way to identify the content of your site.

The META tags we are discussing take the form <meta name="keywords" content= or <meta name="description" content=. Choose keywords wisely, and write a clever title for your Web site. Going back to our HTML exercise, after inserting the META tags our file would look like this...

<html>
<head>
<meta name="keywords" content="antiques collectibles tips Internet buy sell">
<meta name="description" content="Tips for buying antiques and collectibles on the Internet">
<title>ABC Antiques and Collectibles Tips Page</title>
</head>

META Tips

Use as many relevant keywords in your META tags as you can come up with, but don't use the same one over and over in an attempt to get noticed. Most search engines are intelligent enough to know when this is being done, and some will even remove your Web site from their listings if they catch you doing it.

If your description META tag is lengthy, be sure to word it so that the first 40 words are the ones that pack the most punch—some sites limit the amount of words you can use in your description to fifty or less.

Don't use trademarks from other companies in your META tags. There are Web site owners who have faced lawsuits because they used words or phrases within the parameters of their META tags that were trademarked.

Banner Advertising

You've seen them—those banner ads floating across the tops and bottoms of many sites you have visited. How do they work? How much do they cost? Are they worth the cost? Are they for you?

The majority of banner ads appear randomly—that is, if you visit a site and see a banner ad for Old & Older Antiques, leave the site and return a few minutes later, chances are the second visit you would get a different banner ad. It would have the same placement on the page but would be an ad for a different business. Sites that offer the ability to run a search of their pages for certain keywords often tailor their banner advertising to the user by associating certain banner ads with keywords—when a recognized keyword is typed in, the banner ad that is associated with it appears.

How do you get an ad created? Banner ads are basically graphic files—most graphic artists working on computers would know, or be able to figure out, how to create one. In the absence of a graphic artist in the family (or neighborhood), there are an abundance of designers on the Internet ready to help. A good place to visit is the Banner Dudes Ranch (*http://www.bannerdudes.com*) where you can submit your order for a banner ad online and pay as little as $45 for a standard banner or $90 for an animated one. Banner Dudes will redo your ad if you don't like the outcome, and give you two weeks placement on their site if you purchase an ad from them.

Once your ad is created, look for sites with similar interests to what you are promoting. Many of the larger sites have a link for advertising information right on their home pages—if not, look for an e-mail address to contact the Webmaster to find out how you can advertise on the site.

Banner advertising is sold in a variety of ways, including fees for each lead, and in some cases, each click. Be sure you understand the terms of each site you consider for your banner ad, and go for the click-through payment if it is available. This way, you only pay when a Web surfer clicks on your ad, but still get the benefit of having many people who don't click on it see it. Click-through rates are getting harder to find as savvy site owners figure out it isn't the most profitable method for them. Expect to pay as much as $250.00 monthly for your banner ad on a site with high visibility, maybe more.

Did You Say Free?

Yes Virginia, there is free advertising in cyberspace. If your company is making a large commitment to the Internet as the main source of your income, you may want to look into hiring an Internet consultant or ad agency to boost traffic to your site. If you're not ready to take that step, there are still ways to do it yourself.

LinkExchange offers a suite of tools to help do anything from planning to building to promoting your Web site. They offer several programs at reasonable cost to do some of the work for you. What many Web site owners also know is that LinkExchange offers a program that makes it possible to have your banner ad seen on other sites at no cost! The way this is done is that you must display other LinkExchange member ads on your site. For every two ads you display, you earn the right to display your own ad on another site for free. Visit *http://adnetwork.linkexchange.com/index.html* for more details.

Using Reciprocal Links

Another way to promote your site is by the use of *reciprocal links*. Reciprocal links are simply links set up by two different Web sites—your site links to the other site, and that site links to yours. That way, visitors to the other sites in your reciprocal link stable will be only a single click away from coming to yours.

To use this method, you must first contact the Webmaster of the site you would like to link to and get permission. You will usually find an e-mail address on the site home page—if you can't find one for the Webmaster use whatever contact person you can find. Don't be surprised if you sometimes get turned down. There are Webmasters who think that promoting other sites only takes traffic away from their own. Many Webmasters, though, see this as a value-added service to their visitors and are glad to provide reciprocal links. When you reach an agreement with another site for reciprocal links, upload your banner ad to your own server and use the knowledge you acquired in the HTML chapter to write the code and e-mail it to your new friend. The code should look something like this...

```
<a href="http://www.mysite.com"><img src="mybannerad.gif"></a>
```

Business Is Still Business

Most e-mail programs have a feature allowing you to specify some text, or *signature,* at the end of each and every message you send. Use this feature to promote your Web site. A simple message ending statement like "For more information about The ABCs of Making Money on the Internet, visit *http://www.hobbyhouse.com* can be a very effective tool. Many eBay™ buyers have purchased my first book after seeing this very message at the end of the auction confirmation message I sent them.

At the risk of stating the obvious, make sure your Web site address appears in any traditional advertising you do. This includes brochures, press releases, and your business card. Why anybody who spends the time and effort to create their own Web site would not have it prominently displayed on their business card I don't know, but people do it. Maybe they forget. Don't you!

Chapter 7
Traditional Sources for Merchandise

When new dealers get into the antiques and collectibles business, they often do it because they have been collectors themselves and enjoy it immensely. Their collections have been built, over time, with fondness and good memories.

As a collector, price is often not the determining factor in the purchase. The desire to own that elusive piece, or just to complement ones collection, comes above all else. Once that piece is located money is a secondary concern.

This obviously does not work for the dealer, and you must take this into consideration before deciding to pursue antiques and collectibles as a source of income. Most of the items you find at antique malls, both traditional and online, are already priced with little room left for an acceptable profit margin. Online auctions are much the same, with most items selling for close to retail, and in some cases, over retail. Bargains can still be found in all of these places, but many hours will be spent browsing before you find them. In fact, most all of the avenues available to mine for resale items take a lot of time, so you may as well be prepared to spend it. A diversified approach, using as many of the opportunities as you have time for, is the best way to start. You will soon begin to narrow your search to the areas that are most lucrative for you and fit your personality best.

So what is an acceptable profit margin in the antiques and collectibles business? The rule of thumb that has been used for many years is that you should buy at 50% of the retail value of the item you purchase, doubling your money when you sell. Some will say that new dealers should buy at 33% of retail value to afford themselves even more of a safety net. Personally I have found it difficult to buy with any regularity using either rule, and I will purchase an item, especially a small one that requires little effort to carry home and pack for transporting or shipping, if I believe there is a $10-$20 dollar profit to be made. I know an owner/dealer of an antique mall that applies a similar rule to furniture for her booth, buying even large pieces when she believes there is $40-$50 left in the price.

But before you can buy at these slim profit margins, you have to know the market in your area and expected retail on a wide variety of antiques and collectibles. One way to help is by using price guides, and there is certainly no shortage of them available today. You can also use the Internet as a price guide (see Chapter 9—Online Tools to Make It Easy) but unless you carry a laptop computer with a remote Internet connection everywhere you go, you can't check prices while you're standing in a field at an auction. By far, the best way to gain this knowledge is experience, and you only get experience by doing, and occasionally making mistakes.

As you consider these options as sources for acquiring merchandise to sell online, keep in mind that you can also turn the tables and use them as vehicles for selling your merchandise to others who are looking for things to sell online!

Auctions

The best way to find out what other dealers in your area are willing to pay for stock is to regularly attend local auctions. Many people are not aware that even in small communities there is usually at least one auction house that holds weekly sales along with occasional on-site estate sales. While good quality antiques and collectibles do not appear often, they come up regularly enough that you shouldn't overlook this opportunity.

I live in a fairly remote area in the mountains of Western Maryland, an area that is definitely not considered a prosperous one, where you would think good resale items would almost never surface. In just the first two months of 1999 I purchased a World War II lieutenant's uniform, an early Dept. 56 Christmas Village piece, an oak kitchen clock from the late 1800s, an old marble plant stand, several 1940s advertising cards showing "pinup" ladies, and many other treasures, all from local auctions.

One auction in my area is known for not calling out damage on items, so you have to be very careful and be willing to take chances. To compound the problem, there is no *preview* offered with most of the items at this auction. The merchandise is brought to the auction house packed in boxes and that's where it stays until sale time. It is definitely a risky way to buy, and I no longer take chances since a special "antiques and collectibles" auction they held where there was more damaged merchandise than good. Very little of this damage was mentioned by the auctioneer, and quite a few pieces were sent back by high bidders. The auctioneer was obviously annoyed by this, but without the benefit of a preview he has, in my opinion, few options available but to resell returned items with the damage noted. I no longer buy there unless I can inspect the merchandise first.

On the other hand, there is an auction held once or twice a month about two hours' drive from my home. This auctioneer is completely the opposite—every piece is out on display hours before the auction, and damage is called out on every piece he sells. This auctioneer even goes to the trouble of putting even his largest pieces of furniture on a dolly, dragging them to the front of the room, and turning them completely around so that potential buyers can see the front, back, and both sides of a piece before bidding starts. In the case of small items, instead of being delivered to the high bidder they are taken to a wrapping area, where they are efficiently wrapped and packed into boxes that winning bidders pick up at the end of the auction. When you find an auctioneer like this one, hang on with both hands!

If you believe you are getting stuck with bad quality too often, or hear too many horror stories from others attending a particular auction, find another auction house to spend your time and money with. There is always another one nearby, and a bit of extra travel may be well worth it to have an auctioneer who thoroughly checks his merchandise and notes damage before the bidding begins.

Here's a quick overview for attending a typical auction. Before even leaving the house you can perform some of the most important functions: load up your car or truck with price guides, boxes, and newspaper for wrapping, and unless you know good food will be available, pack a lunch so you can outlast the competition. Comfortable shoes are a good idea too, in case you can't find a seat. Better yet, take your own chair.

Try to arrive at least an hour early and take a quick look around at the items being offered. Most auction houses will have them displayed on tables and expect bidders to inspect things closely before the auction starts. If you see items you are interested in, find the registration table and get a number. You cannot bid at an auction without a number, and all that is usually required to get one is to hand the registrar your drivers license. They will record your name and address, ask you for your phone number, and issue you a card with a number on it. This number is how you will be identified for the remainder of the auction. If you don't already know the payment terms, ask now. Some auctions take cash and personal checks only, some also accept credit cards. Still others won't accept checks unless you are "known" to the auction house, or unless you have a "bank letter of credit" to present to them. While I respect the right of an auction house to protect themselves from fraudulent buyers, I am offended by the bank letter of credit and do not participate in auctions that require them. In fact, I consider them to be somewhat of a joke, as anybody with a computer and scanner can forge a bank letter on "official" bank stationery nowadays.

Also inquire about buyer's premium at this time. Some auction houses are imposing what they call a "buyer's premium" on merchandise, and you have to take this into consideration when purchasing. Often the premium is 10%, so paying a $100 high bid for an item actually costs you $110. Buyer's premium is another volatile topic that I won't address here. You can make up your own mind if it's worth it to you or not. Auctioneers that use it say it helps them to get top quality merchandise; however my experience has been that there are still plenty of excellent auctions around that don't impose one.

If you're so inclined, and I highly recommend you do this if you're new at this game, take paper and pencil and make the rounds again, noting the items you are interested in. If you're not sure of retail value, make a trip back to your vehicle and search through the price guides you brought with you. If you can't find an item, make a guess as to retail value. Across from your item listings, write all of the retail values in one column, and in another column write the most you are willing to pay for that item. Then stick to your list. Better to come home with nothing more than experience than to overpay. Overpaying for stock is the most common mistake a beginning dealer makes.

Now, return to the auction hall and find a seat, if you can. It's going to be a long day and you'll get tired standing. As the bidding gets underway, watch to see how it's done. Usually the auctioneer starts out the bidding at a price that nobody reacts to. He will then drop the opening bid lower, and lower, and sometimes even lower. Finally, somebody will raise their hand, and they're off! It can be hard to follow, so if this is your first time it's best to sit, watch, and study for awhile before placing your first bid. I have been to hundreds of auctions, and I still watch and study before bidding when attending a new auction house for the first time.

Don't get discouraged if the first item or two that you were interested in goes sky high. You never know the reasons for this—it could be two family members that couldn't decide on how to divide the estate who are both after the same piece and mad as hell. It could even be a dealer buying something for a spouse and willing to go way higher than he or she usually would. If there are a lot of collectors at the auction, there's a chance you will come home empty handed. But always remember that each time you attend an auction, even if you buy nothing, you are gaining experience and knowledge. This is well worth the hours you invest sitting and watching.

Yard Sales

Yes, yard sales! Some will tell you that yard sales are a waste of time, the gain not being worth the effort. Admittedly the good finds are few and far between, but don't rule them out. Especially if you spend Friday and/or Saturday mornings relaxing, why not take a lazy drive and hunt for bargains.

I have a yard sale story for you, and I know this one to be true because it happened to me. I was driving along a back road to avoid a congested Interstate highway one Saturday morning when I saw that wonderful "Yard Sale Ahead" sign. It was a small sale, and after just a few minutes I had scanned the tables and was getting ready to depart. For whatever reason, I took a second look at a bowl of fruit—the fruits were actually plush toys. Suddenly I froze in my tracks as I realized the bowl under the pile of fruit was depression glass. I probably missed it on my first scan because it was off-white, not the usual pink, green, blue or yellow that most of us consider to be "depression". Closer inspection revealed that the bowl was American Sweetheart Monax, and while I didn't know the exact value, at $2.00 I knew it was a good buy.

But what's this? Another bowl of plush fruit! Could it be? Yes, indeed, another American Sweetheart Monax bowl. I inspected both bowls for chips and cracks and handed the seller $4. Later that day I looked up this bowl in a price guide, and the value was listed at $60 each. Upon asking around I found out that it was not an easy item to find, and I already knew that American Sweetheart Monax was a popular pattern, at least in my end of the world. I had no trouble selling both bowls within a few days at $60 each. One of the bowls was bought by a dealer who knew a collector willing to pay even a higher price.

The most interesting part of the story, at least to me, is that when I paid the yard sale seller the $4 I also handed her the fruit back and told her I was only interested in the bowls and she could have the fruit to sell again. She was mystified, and could not figure out why someone would want these bowls and not the plush fruit!

We're learning about the Internet as a part of your antiques and collectibles business, but here's a traditional tip that even many well-seasoned dealers don't use: you can also hold yard sales as part of your overall business plan. It is not uncommon for a well-advertised yard sale stocked with some quality collectibles (and a few antiques for good measure) to net the seller a tidy $1000 over a weekend. It's also a good way to get rid of household items you "inherit" when buying box lots at auction.

Yard sales have become such a popular way to make money that books have been written about them. It's not rocket science—just remember to price items according to what *you* would expect to pay at a yard sale. Clean up your items as best as you can, and if possible set up the night before and cover everything—early birds are pretty much a given, even if you state in the ad they aren't welcome. Put price tags on everything, and start this process well in advance of the sale. You'll be surprised how long it takes to get everything in order.

I have a suggestion for those of you who really don't want early birds walking around while you are trying to get set up in the morning. Put a line in your ad stating that to deter early shoppers any merchandise sold before the advertised starting time will be marked up 300%. If they still show up at least you will be compensated for it!

You'll notice I referred to a "well-advertised" yard sale—your ad is your most important tool so make sure you don't skimp on the cost. List as many of your sale items in the ad as you possibly can to attract the largest group with the most diverse tastes. Post as many street signs as possible to attract passing motorists.

Flea Markets

Flea markets happen every weekend in every state, and come in almost any size you can think of. Some are nothing more than a few tables set up in a church parking lot. Others are immense—like the thousands of dealers who set up each weekend at the Rose Bowl Flea Market in Southern California. Any of them can be a good source of resale items.

Renninger's Extravaganzas are well known and well worth the trip—find out more at *http://www.renningers.com*. There are many other flea markets lesser known but just as large. A good online source to find a flea market near you is *http://www.fleamarketguide.com*, where you will find well-organized listings for markets all over the country plus a few in

Canada. They even provide a link to the weather forecast in the area you plan to visit so you can find out if you'll need your rain gear!

Like yard sales, don't overlook flea markets as a source for selling if you enjoy the atmosphere and don't mind rolling out of bed at 4 AM, distance driving, and setting up and tearing down your space all in one day. You can usually secure a space without a reservation if you arrive early enough, and the cost is very reasonable compared to renting a space at an antiques and collectibles show. It's not for everybody, but there are definitely people making money doing it.

Shows

What about antiques and collectibles shows? Can bargains be found there? The simple answer is "yes" there are always sleepers hiding at every show. The reality is that you need a very finely tuned eye and broad range of expertise to find those sleepers on a regular basis, especially at what I call "upscale" shows. When you walk into a show and see primarily high-end glassware or 18th century furniture, you can expect the dealers know what they have and are priced at what the market will bear. Investing in this high-end merchandise is not wise unless you have a source of ready buyers for it, or do upscale shows yourself. For the majority of the general line dealers who fill the antique malls of America, this just isn't a viable way to buy.

There are plenty of shows that are full of merchandise worth investigating, though. You can pretty much guess that an outdoor show will be interesting—some resemble flea markets more than shows and are filled with buying opportunities. The famous Brimfield shows are like this, and in fact some people do refer to Brimfield as a market.

Shows can be an educational experience, and you get to see things that just don't appear in antique malls. The good buys that do exist are often swapped before the gates open, dealer-to-dealer, and marked up before the public arrives. In fact, dealers buying from other dealers is what keeps this business alive, with some items trading hands three, four, and even more times between dealers before finally landing in the hands of the collector.

Shows are fun, especially for the collector. As a dealer, I don't go to shows expecting to find a truck full of good buys. That way I'm not as disappointed if nothing of resale merit turns up. Don't count upscale shows out altogether, but for finding resale merchandise I would put them near the bottom of my list.

Your Attic and Basement

Don't laugh! Most of us have watched *The Antiques Roadshow* or other related programming and know that many people have found items in their own homes worth tidy sums of money. As you fine tune your eye at finding valuables, you might even discover some of your own things from childhood, relegated to shoe boxes years ago, that now command prices in the hundreds of dollars. Don't expect to come up with the lavish finds you see on *The Antiques Roadshow,* but even your old 35mm camera that you replaced a few years back is probably worth something to somebody. You can often find that somebody on the Internet. And so we come to **Ray's Rule #1:** *if you haven't used it for six months, you probably don't need it.* My wife heartily disagrees.

Private Homes

This used to be one of the best ways for experienced antiques dealers to buy. Countless hours were spent coming up with ways to be the first one in the door when a death or divorce would occur. Today, with the Internet and the *Antiques Roadshow,* sellers are much more educated. They often want retail value and higher for their property because they know what it's worth (or at least think they do) and are sentimentally attached to it. I have heard of several dealers who have sworn off buying this way because of too many experiences where the seller simply would not settle for anything less than a price that would be considered strong even in the retail market.

We, however, are leaving no stone unturned, and this can still be a very lucrative way to add to your stock if you work hard at it. Begin by placing an ad in your local newspaper identifying yourself as a *cash buyer* for antiques and collectibles. Be prepared to run your ad daily for extended periods of time—it may be worth your while to explore the cost of running your ad continuously. Repetitious exposure is paramount in this game.

Second in importance to your ad is your ability to screen out good prospects from those not worth your time. Seller intent is the most important thing to establish—be sure you are not being "used" for a free appraisal. Once in the house, if the subject of appraisal comes up, it is best to offer to provide one for a fee and to make sure the seller understands you will then let the buying to other dealers. That way you avoid conflict of interest problems while still making some money. Often, though, the seller will decline the paid appraisal, leaving you to negotiate with them for the contents of the house.

You should also ask questions to find out the type of antiques and collectibles the seller has. If they have only furniture, and you don't deal in or know much about furniture, you should politely bow out of the transaction. Or they might have items that are more suited for a yard sale than a spot in your online antique mall booth. The first time I was invited into someone else's home to make an offer on some "collectibles" I arrived to hear the seller tell me stories of how she had contacted others and "nobody even wanted to bother coming out to look at my things." I soon found out why—even though there was a basement full of boxes and the boxes were full of items this person treasured, there was absolutely nothing worth more than a few dollars at a yard sale, if you could sell it at all. Everyone else she contacted apparently had asked the right questions first, and I learned quickly after that experience.

Last but not least, find out if the seller has an idea of the retail value of their items. If they do, ask how they determined that value and how close to their estimate the asking price is. If necessary, explain to them that as a dealer you cannot pay retail, and if that's what they expect to get they should run an ad in the classified section of their local newspaper to try to sell what they have themselves. Most times if a seller is hoping for retail you don't stand a chance—usually their idea of retail is already higher than yours and you will only insult them with an offer, even one you consider to be generous. It's better to be honest right at the beginning and not waste your time.

If you are lucky enough to stumble onto a house full of good antiques and a seller who seems to be a good prospect, try to get the seller to name a price first. **Ray's Rule #2:** *the first one to name a price usually comes out on the short end of the negotiations.* However if the seller, after cheerful prodding from you, absolutely refuses to name a price, you must take the initiative and do so. Make your offer on an entire group of items, offering 50% of retail on only the best ones, the sure sellers, as your opening price for the entire group. This should be a safe starting point if further negotiating ensues.

When you've finally established a price you can work with, pay cash immediately and ask for a signed receipt. Remove the items from the house immediately—if you make arrangements to pick up and pay the next day, often the seller has time to consider the sale and talk with friends who will tell him what a bad deal he made. When you return the seller has changed his mind, and you've not only wasted your time, you've lost out on a good deal to boot.

Here's one final tip about buying from private homes that surprises even experienced dealers but yet seems obvious when you think about it. Many dealers, especially the ones who work very hard for little money (which is the majority of us, by the way), are intimidated by people with wealth. They have been swayed by stories of rich people being rich because they pinch every penny. They've heard that people with money are, in many ways, thriftier than the average low- or middle-income wage earner—how do you think they got so rich? The fact is that most people with money are not as concerned about getting top dollar for their merchandise than somebody who needs the money is. When you live paycheck-to-paycheck and acquire something of value, chances are you will not let it go until you get top dollar for it, unless you are having financial problems of some kind. People of means have better merchandise, and are often willing to let it go at better prices simply because money is not a problem for them.

Consignment

If handled correctly, consignment can be another tool to add to your arsenal. Consignment is simply accepting merchandise from other people to sell on their behalf, with the understanding that you receive a fee upon completion of the sale.

A typical consignment entails the seller telling you what their minimum acceptable price for the item is. You then mark the item up 50%, hopefully sell it at that price, and keep the difference. With the advent of the Internet auction, is has become relatively easy to dispose of merchandise in a timely manner with little overhead, so you can plug in whatever percentage markup you feel comfortable with and set your reserve price accordingly. Remember to figure in the fees that are associated with selling online, typically a listing fee based on your reserve price or starting bid, and a percentage of the final price. Also consider you/your business will have to pay taxes on the sale, so mark up consignment merchandise to cover all of these expenses plus a commission.

It is wise to draw up a consignment contract that spells out the details of the transaction and have it signed by both you and the consignee. It doesn't have to be fancy—you can generate something from your own computer. The contract should contain the inventory number you assign the item, a description, the date you received it from the consignee, and the length of the contract (90 days is typical), and your fee. A clause giving you the right to reduce the price of the item after a specified amount of time is recommended.

Antique Malls

Some of my best finds have been made in antique malls. Malls are full of general line dealers, and any experienced dealer will tell you that it is absolutely impossible to be knowledgeable about every type of antique or collectible. Consequently, there are still enough items that "slip through" and end up being priced way above retail—or become steals waiting to be harvested by a dealer or collector with knowledge of what it is.

Price guides, while being generally useful in making all of us more aware and educated, have greatly reduced the amount of "good finds" hiding in antique malls. Some prices, depression glass being a good example, have become so standardized that you will see the same price on the same pieces no matter where you go. And with new price guides being published seemingly every day, it might seem futile to walk the aisles of antique malls when today's dealers have all of this information at their fingertips. Rest assured it is not futile, and the antique malls in your area should be a regular stop on your buying list.

Second Hand Stores

Don't spend a lot of time browsing second hand stores, but on occasion a good find will turn up at one. It doesn't happen often, but the good news is that when it does the owner usually doesn't know what he or she has and will sell it for well below market value. Rural areas seem to be better known for treasures appearing than larger cities, probably because not as much traffic (i.e. dealers) passes through. If you're on your way to an antique mall near closing time and pass a second hand store, keep going. Otherwise, put on the brakes and take a look.

Importers/Wholesalers

Several companies import European antiques and offer them for sale to dealers. While much of their inventory is large furniture, which is more difficult to sell on the Internet due to packing and shipping costs (not to mention you have to have space to store it until it sells), they also handle smalls and diminutive furniture.

Jere's Antiques, Inc.
Jere's has one of the largest stocks of English antiques in America and specializes in Victorian pine.
9 North Jefferson Street
Savannah, Georgia
Phone: (912) 236-2815
Fax: (912) 236-0274

The Green Door, Inc.
The Green Door has regular tag sales of container lots of old furniture and antiques. Dealer resale numbers are needed to participate in the sale.
2100 East Kivett Drive
High Point, NC
Phone: 1-800-775-3434
Fax: (336) 889-5128

Exporters

There are several good sources for antiques from England and Europe if you are interested in specializing and are willing to buy quantity. 20- and 40-foot containers are common sizes, with 40-foot containers generally costing from $8,000 to $100,000 depending on the type and quality of merchandise you select. Shipping is done by steamship.

Charles International Antiques
London Road Wrotham (A20) Kent TN 157RR
Phone: 011-44-1732-823654
Fax: 011-44-1732-824484
e-mail: c.bremner@antiques2.demon.co.uk
http://www.collect.com/charles

Global Antiques Holland
Grathermerweg 47A, Kelpen, Holland
Phone: 01131-495-651239
Fax: 01131-495-651993
e-mail: global@global-antiques.com
http://www.global-antiques.com

Millennium 2000 Antiques
Phone: +44 780-8428252
Fax: +44 1352-720197
e-mail: info@millennium-antiques.co.uk
http://www.millennium-antiques.co.uk

Wigan Antique Center
Phone: 011-44-1942-241484
Fax: 001-44-1942-234412
e-mail: jcollins37@compuserve.com
http://ourworld.compuserve.com/homepages/jcollins37

Young's Antiques
Showroom, Offices, and Warehouse at:
Calceto Farm,
Units 1 & 2
Lyminster, West Sussex, England
Telephone: 011-44-1903-889566
e-mail: YAexport@aol.com
http://www.youngsantiques.zetnet.co.uk/

Reproductions and Giftware

As an antiques "purist" I hesitate to even talk about reproductions. However, this book is about making money, and there is mounting evidence that the reproductions and gift markets can be lucrative for dealers who choose to specialize in those categories. Several good wholesalers exist for buying furniture, porcelain, glassware, and many other items that are manufactured overseas and shipped in quantity for resale in America.

If you choose to explore this market and plan to sell out of antique malls as well as online, don't make the mistake of mixing quality antiques in your booth with reproductions. Many antique buyers are turned off by this, and will shy away from your good merchandise. If you choose to handle reproductions, rent a separate space in the same mall if you must, but don't mix. Handle the reproductions as a separate business altogether.

Finding merchandise to sell is as easy as shopping from a catalog or browsing online, but you'll have to be a dealer with a tax resale number. If you don't currently have a resale number, visit your nearest antiques and collectibles shop or mall and ask the dealers there how to go about getting one in your state.

One of the biggest drawbacks of dealing in reproductions and giftware is that catalogs can be deceiving. If you (or perhaps you remember your parents doing this) have ever ordered clothing from a catalog, only to have your slacks arrive and be the most awful looking things you've ever seen, you know what I mean. This is not to say that the reproductions in the catalogs I'm going to tell you about are low quality—most are not. But it is immensely helpful to visit the showrooms of these sources if at all possible. Not only do you get a better feel for what you're investing your money in, the selection is greater and there are items in the showrooms that do not make it into the catalogs.

A.A. Importing Company
Dealers can call toll free to get on a mailing list. Catalogs cost $10.00 which is redeemable with your first order over $100.00. A.A. offers four different showroom/warehouse facilities in St. Louis, MO, San Francisco, CA, Edison, NJ, and Swedesboro, NJ.
Phone: 1-800-325-0602
e-mail: info@aaimporting.com
http://www.aaimporting.com

Castle Antiques and Reproductions
You can get a free catalog from Castle by sending a business card to...
Castle Antiques & Reproductions, Inc.
515 Welwood Avenue
Hawley, PA 18428
For directions and hours call (717) 226-8550.
Castle also has an online catalog you can browse at *http://www.castleantiques.com*

Fred & Dottie's, Inc.
Fred and Dottie's, Inc. charges $1.00 for their brochure package, which is refundable with your first order. Send your business card and $1.00 to...
Fred & Dottie's Inc.
6711 Perkiomen Avenue
Birdsboro, PA 19508
For directions and hours call (610) 582-1506.

CHAPTER 8
Online Sources for Merchandise

Online Auctions

The best known online auction at this point in time is eBay™, and you can routinely find over two million (yes, two million!) items up for bid at any given time. Not all of these are antique and collectibles, but you can certainly deal in other niche markets and make money selling giftware, consumer electronics, etc.

eBay™ was commanding very high prices during its first few years of existence. I believe this was, at least in part, due to the fact that the first online auction users were computer literate but not necessarily antiques and collectibles literate. With this fascinating new medium placed before them, they became instant dealers, collectors, and auctioneers without first learning the nuances of this market that take years to acquire. They purchased with more regard to possession than price. The novelty of this new way of buying enticed some to overbid, and many experienced auction frenzy for the first time, which also fueled higher prices.

This trend started to change in late 1998 and continues to evolve. As people gain more experience, the novelty of buying this way is beginning to wear off. But the biggest event to level the playing field has been the increased numbers of experienced dealers and collectors who have started to use the online auctions. Their wisdom is price-correcting this venue, and prices realized online are becoming more in line with what the overall market can bear.

If you are unfamiliar with using online auctions, especially if you're a dealer, I urge you to get involved. You can find a list of the best known ones in Appendix A of this book. There are many compelling reasons to sell using them, not the least of which is that you get your cash in a short amount of time. If you set a fair reserve price and are selling good quality merchandise, your item will usually sell. Most people run their auction seven days, and expect payment within ten days of auction close. You can realistically expect to turn items over and get cash-in-hand within 2-3 weeks of listing them. The icing on the cake: online auction fees are but a small fraction of what your local auctioneer will charge you.

For complete details on using online auctions and getting the most out of them, run right to your computer and point your browser to *http://www.hobbyhouse.com* for my companion book to the one you are reading, **The ABCs of Collecting Online**. If you don't have a computer yet, call 1-800-554-1447 to order-this book also tells you how to buy a computer and find the best deal from an Internet Service Provider if you're just starting out.

Online Antique Malls

What could be more relaxing and fun for a dealer or collector than browsing through an antique mall from your living room? You can, and while purists may bemoan not being able to physically pick up and touch their purchases, Internet photos can suffice for many. This is one of the most neglected opportunities on the Internet-everyone is so caught up in the online auctions that the malls are being overlooked, and therefore bargains are being overlooked also. Online malls are also great for those dealers who have customers looking for a special item-an item that you probably wouldn't come across without access to the Internet. Offering an antique search service has never been easier, and this can be a value added feature of your business.

Appendix A contains a list of virtual malls for your shopping pleasure, so start pointing and clicking!

Online Individual Dealers & WebRings

Some of the finest antiques available online are in the hands of individual dealers, but with the vastness of the Internet it is difficult to locate many of them. One of the creative ways being used to deal with this problem is WebRings, and you can find several good ones for individual dealers at *http://www.webring.org*. Simply type "antique" into the search box on their home page and then click the search button. You will get a listing of WebRings specializing in anything from general antiques to dolls to antique outboard motors.

You can also visit *http://computrends.com/antiquering.html* for the self-proclaimed "Best Antiques and Collectibles Site on the Web". The home page offers a brief tutorial on how to navigate the site, and you can then start visiting different antiques Web pages with one click of your mouse.

http://www.webring.org

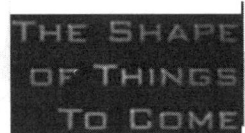

Welcome to WebRing, one of the fastest and most exciting ways to navigate the World Wide Web! This completely free service offers easy access to hundreds of thousands of member websites organized by related interests into easy-to-travel Rings.

You can find Rings that interest you by clicking on category links in the RingWorld Directory, or by using RingSearch.

WebRing is one of the simplest and most efficient ways to find content on the Internet. Our member sites are everywhere. Anytime you find yourself at a WebRing member page, just click on the navigation buttons or hypertext links to travel to other sites in the Ring.

Any web site owner can apply to join an existing Ring or create a new Ring. Rings may be listed in the RingWorld Directory once they contain at least five sites.

STATUS REPORT

TERMS OF SERVICE

WEBRING PRIVACY NOTICE

Search for: ○ Any Word ● All Words ○ Exact Phrase
In: ☑ Ring Descriptions ☑ Ring Names & Keywords

[Search]

RingWorld, the WebRing Directory

Arts and Humanities
Artists ¤ Family ¤ Countries and Cultures ¤ Design Arts
Education ¤ Literature ¤ Music ¤ Museums and Galleries

http://computrends.com/antiquering.html

AWARDS:

Links² Go Key Resource
Collectibles Topic

Showcase Gallery

Selected highlights
from the AntiqueRing:

Courtesy of: . . . . . .
Tri-State Antiques™

Welcome to the BEST Antiques & Collectibles Sites on the Web!™ You are about to embark on a tour of select premium antique sites offering a wide range of antiques and collectibles for the discerning buyer. Other sites along the way offer top-quality reference information, tips, and will serve to educate you about various topics. You will see some of the most outstanding antiques available on the internet, and prices will be shown. You won't have to be telephoning to find out what something costs only to find out it's beyond your budget! All of our members proudly display their merchandise with prices listed . . . and NO reproductions are permitted.

NEWCOMERS: To learn how to follow the trail of antique sites that belong to the antiquering, click here.

REPEAT VISITORS: If you already know how to surf the AntiqueRing, you may begin your tour of the BEST Antiques & Collectibles Sites on the Web! by clicking below:

http://www.circline.com.

HELLO, VISITOR.
Welcome to CIRCLINE!

Circline brings an extraordinary collection of thousands of fine antiques from highly renowned dealers across the globe directly to you. You are invited to shop across time, distance, cultures and tastes in this incredibly varied marketplace. Search for the antique you have always wanted. Browse through your favorite styles. Discover something timeless.

 **REGISTER**

Please register for free to enjoy all of Circline's features. Our quick, confidential registration gives you your own Portfolio, access to the useful Request service, the ability to buy and place holds, and much more.

 **FEATURED INVENTORY**

Hercules

Circline heartily welcomes summer with a superb selection of **Antique Garden Ornaments**. Featured this month are statuary, urns, fountains, garden furniture, and more. <u>Click here</u> to view the collection. And while you're at it, pick up a few tips on caring for antique garden ornaments, and see how your decorative arts library stacks up to Hayden-Fandetta's scholarly bibliography.

 **JOURNAL**

Circline's Journal is a new feature catering to the interests of both novice and connoisseur alike. Whether you're looking for an insightful exhibition review, a scholarly topical article, or entertaining tidbits falling somewhere in between - the Journal promises to evolve into all that and more.

Zelfportret
1613-14

Van Dyck 1599 - 1641
at Koninklijke Museum voor Schone Kunsten, Antwerp, Belgium till 15th August then at Royal Academy of Arts, London, UK from 11th September - 10th December 1999

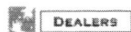 **LOG IN**

Current Circline members: Please login here.

Email Address
Password

Log In

DEALERS

Circline has joined with the most prestigious dealers in the world to create the online antique marketplace. Each dealer is carefully selected by Circline for their expertise, integrity, and reputation. When you use Circline, you will gain tremendously from their knowledge and experience, and can be confident in the authenticity of the available antiques.

EDUCATION

Just as Circline is the best resource for you to find antiques, it is also a wonderful place to learn about them. To complement the extensive collection of pictures and information in our catalog, and the hundreds of years of collective authority of our dealers, Circline introduces our new Education section.

http://www.rubylane.com.

Ray, Welcome back to **Ruby Lane**™
Bringing You the World of Antiques, Collectibles *&* Fine Art

Tue, August 10th

Giveaway
Ray, you're all set to win great prizes all this month! See how

Start Here
How do I find, buy, and sell?
Tell a friend, win a prize!

Auction Counters
Use our FREE Auction Counter in your auctions.

Be an Affiliate
Join today and earn $$$$!

Our Stats
1,861,916 items in Global Search!
2,000 Catalogs!
1,025,000 hits a week!

Corporate Member
ACDA Antique & Collectibles Dealer Association, Inc.

Search

Catalogs
Help

Look what they're saying about us!
....
"I think your site is the best, inclusive of most locations. Never have trouble loading it. Keep up the good work!!!"
J.P.

Antiques   Collectibles   Fine Art   Global Search
Courtyard   Help   Site Map   Contact Us   About Us
Privacy Policy   Auction Counter

Member of the BEST Antiques & Collectibles Sites on the Web!
[Next site] [Go]

Hot Shops
Trojan Horse Antiques & Collectibles
Come On In... You Never Know What's Inside!

Evans Collectables
Vintage Compacts, Purses, Lighters and More

Chan's Stamp Corner
Chinese Stamps and Coins

All Shops
Complete shop directory for Antiques & Collectibles & Fine Art

Our lawyer says Copyright (c) 1998-1999 Ruby Lane (tm). All Rights Reserved.

WebRings link a multitude of sites together; when you are finished examining one you simply use the WebRing link to get to another. If you want to efficiently surf the Internet for individual dealers and/or information on a particular category, this is the way to go. If you decide to create an online storefront, or already have one, consider enrolling with one of the existing WebRings for more exposure, or start a new one specializing in your area of expertise. Both of these options are available from the webring.org site.

One site you should visit if you're looking for the finest of the fine in antiques is *http://www.circline.com*. Many quality dealers list their merchandise here, and you can easily spend $10,000 with one click of the mouse. You won't find a $250.00 Seth Thomas mantel clock, but if you're interested in a Fine French Empire Bronze Dore Mantel Clock and have $15,000 to spend, you'll find it here.

Online Catalogs

One of the most interesting and useful sites on the Internet for antiques and collectibles can be found at *http://www.rubylane.com*. This site is evolving rapidly, and might be classified by some as an online antique mall. But it is much more.

Ruby Lane offers a global search engine, which looks not just for a specific auction or mall site but will return results from several locations. In other words, if you run a search from eBay™, you will get results of only items listed with eBay™. When you run a search from Ruby Lane, it will return results from The Internet Antique Store (http://www.tias.com), AntiqueNet (http: //www.antiquenet.com), and a host of other top Internet sites.

You can also open your own storefront at Ruby Lane. The proprietors are making a real effort to keep the Antiques and Fine Arts section a high quality place to shop, allowing only genuine items 100+ years old (no reproductions) to qualify as antiques. Alternately, you can open a collectibles shop, with the requirement there being that the merchandise is at least 20 years old, of high quality, and not a reproduction. A very reasonable 10% commission on sales is charged, and there is no setup fee. Adding to the credibility of this site, it requires terms that I have long hoped online auction sites would use-you must post a return policy before they will allow you to open your shop.

The process for registering and creating/opening your own store is amazingly easy, and once done you are added to the global search engine. If you use another venue besides Ruby Lane to sell, visitors using the Ruby Lane global search engine will find your other items too.

At the risk of sounding like an advertisement for this innovative company, here is the information, taken directly from their site, as to the costs associated with selling on Ruby Lane:

- There are no setup fees.
- Ruby Lane has Art & Antiques shops and Collectibles shops. A $250 refundable deposit is used toward commission fees in the Art & Antique section to help ensure that these shops are selling at a higher price point.

There is no deposit required to open a shop in the Collectibles section.

- 10% commission is charged on all items sold from your Ruby Lane shop.
- New dealers receive a special start-up incentive -- your first sale is commission-free so you can be totally comfortable with our services before spending any money.
- For $200 we will create a logo to be displayed on your Ruby Lane shop pages.
- If you do not want to create computer images from photos or do not have this capability, we charge $2 dollars per photo.
- If you would like us to input your items into shop from information you provide us, we charge $2 per item.
- If you want an active link from your Ruby Lane shop to another web site, we charge $25 per month per unique link for this service.
- There are no other charges.

Antiques and Collectibles Bulletin Boards

Another way to hone in on merchandise is to bookmark a few bulletin boards that specialize in antiques and collectibles, or to find some that specialize in your particular area of interest. Bulletin boards, or message boards as some call them, are Web sites where you can post a message that anyone else accessing that site can see. The bulletin board software usually will automatically generate a link that others can click on to e-mail you, and some allow you to add the URL of a Web page you want to direct them to. You can browse for bulletin boards that interest you buy typing "bulletin board" into the search box of your favorite Internet search engine.

Here's one example of how selling on a bulletin board works. You bought a box lot at auction, wanting the piece of Fiestaware that was in it. There are a few yard sale items in the box also, but they're only worth $5-$10 each.

You could list the items on eBay™, starting the bidding at $5.00, but does that really make sense? The minimal $0.25 listing fee amounts to 5% of the cost of a $5.00 item, and if it sells another 5% is taken. Even if you're an experienced and proficient eBay™ user, you'll spend 15-30 minutes taking a photo, downloading it to your computer, uploading it to your server, writing a description, and filling out the eBay™ listing form. That's a good half-hour invested for a $4.50 profit-IF the item sells. Add to that the aggravation caused by **Ray's Rule** #3: Online auction bidders for yard sale quality items are 4-5 times as likely to default on payment than bidders for genuine antiques and collectibles.

If you don't want to bother with a traditional yard sale, why not try listing the items on a collectibles bulletin board! It's free, and while successful selling at online auctions requires a photo, in this venue photos aren't a necessity. You go to your favorite bulletin board, click on Post a Message, and your message can be as simple as "collectible pocket knives for sale-$5 or less. E-mail me for more details". If you have no takers, you've only wasted a few minutes and can still list your items with an online auction if you'd like. Hopefully, after a few e-mail messages back and forth to prospective buyers, you'll be shipping out your pocket knives.

Of course, you can just use the bulletin boards to buy. I have had both good and bad experiences buying through bulletin boards. I got a great deal on some price guides that were almost brand new, but got burned on a silver plate teapot, advertised as "mint", that arrived with a bent finial, broken handle, and several dents that were obviously not shipping damage. Make sure you ask all the right questions before buying from a bulletin board seller-many are inexperienced and are using the boards because they don't have the time or knowledge to get involved in selling through the online auctions. Ask for a photo-the seller may not have the capability to send you an electronic one, but at least you've asked. Some bulletin boards will not allow dealers to list merchandise-they are reserved for sharing information only. Respect these rules and find another board to do your selling from.

Antiques and Collectibles Newsgroups

As a source of information and a way to meet collectors with similar interests, newsgroups are hard to beat-if you find a good one. There are also frequent posts about items for sale in most antiques and collectibles newsgroups, so it can be another way to buy and sell.

The down side to newsgroups is that you need to be thick skinned to participate on some of them. Self-proclaimed "experts" congregate and aren't shy about running newcomers out of town on a rail if they post a message that doesn't sit well with the group that fancies itself in control. I subscribed to an antiques newsgroup some time back and watched as a select group mercilessly destroyed anybody with an opinion different from theirs. Needless to say, I didn't stay subscribed very long.

Newsgroups work in conjunction with your e-mail program, which explains why they are described by some as a marriage of bulletin boards and e-mail. If you've read my companion book, ***The ABCs of Collecting Online***, you've already asked the right questions and have an Internet Service Provider that gives you access to all newsgroups, and you've learned a bit about newsgroup etiquette. You can post messages and reply to posts of others, or in some cases, contact them using their personal e-mail account. If you don't know how to access them, launch your e-mail software and search for "Newsgroups" in the help menu. Or point your browser to *http://www.deja.com* where you can run a search for discussion groups and communities that echo your interests.

Here are some general newsgroups to check out, but if you end up getting flamed just remember that I warned you!

alt.antiques.delaware.joe
alt.collecting
alt.forsale
alt.marketplace.collectables
pdaxs.ads.antiques
rec.antiques.marketplace
rec.collecting

Online Classified Ads

Classified ads are one of the few linear ways of doing business that, based on the quantity of them, seem to have made a successful transformation to the Internet. Browsing classifieds online is a bit easier than thumbing through pages, as most sites that offer them also offer a search engine to enter keyword(s) instead of having to scroll through all listings.

Antique Week posts all of the classified ads appearing in their publication every Monday, free of charge to advertisers. While no search engine is provided, you can use the Find option under the Edit menu of your browser to locate specific word(s). Point your browser to *http://www.antiqueweek.com/awclass.htm* for the Antique Week classified ads.

Antique Trader also offers classified advertisers the option of having any size classified ad that runs in their publication also appear on the Internet for an extra $1.00 per week. You can browse them for free by visiting *http://www.collect.com/antiquetrader/buysell.html* and either view all listings or search by keyword(s).

Krause Publications puts out over 30 magazines on collectibles, and all of their magazines offer classified ads. The ads are available for browsing online, by keyword search and/or by magazine, at *http://www.collectit.net/index.html*.

Here are some sites that offer you the opportunity to post free classified ads. In order to be free, the tradeoff is that you will be inundated with banner advertising on these sites. If you don't want to take a chance on an item not selling at an auction, or want to hunt for bargains in a non-auction environment, give these a look.

http://www.interking.com
http://classifieds.yahoo.com
http://www.freeclassifieds.com

Flea Market Merchandise

There is a ready source of flea market merchandise available online from businesses that specialize in closeouts and wholesale selling. If you want to deal in new clothing, toys, perfume and other flea market items, here are some good places to look.

Merchandise USA (*http://www.merchandiseusa.com*) has a 30,000 square foot warehouse located in Chicago, Illinois and has been doing business since 1984. Specializing in wide variety of consumer and gift items, the minimum quantities you can purchase are typically anywhere from 10- to 50-dozen of one thing. Follow the link from their home page to their current inventory to view the merchandise they have available, which varies on a regular basis. You'll find photo albums, toys, porcelain dolls and figures, books, clothing, and much more.

Wholesale prices for brand name colognes, perfumes, and cosmetics are available from Paris Fragrance (*http://www.paris-fr.com*). This company is located in Arlington, Texas and doing business since 1988. Paris offers discount pricing for many of the top brand names as well as brands inspired by the originals.

Cherished Teddies, Precious Moments, and other items like dolls, tools, sports collectibles, and toys can be found at the Bargain Supply Company (*http://www.bargain-mall.com/bargains/index.html*). Most items can be purchased in quantity, and the minimum order is $100.

If computers and electronics are more to your liking, Surplus Traders (*http://www.73.com*) may be of help. Surplus Traders is an online wholesale distributor and clearing house for surplus electronic, computer, and other equipment. From network components to video cards, you'll find it here-discounted!

T. L. Merchandise (*http://www.tlmerchandise.com*) is based in East Orange, New Jersey and offers discounted prices for crystal, porcelain, stone, and other gift items. Unlike sellers who specialize in closeouts, T. L. Merchandise does not require quantity purchases or minimum orders.

For a wide variety of flea market items including tee-shirts, toys, novelty items, magic tricks and much more at wholesale prices visit Salt Lake City, Nevada based Novel-Tees Wholesale (*http://www.novel-tees.com*). Add your selections to an online shopping cart and check out via secure server, or pay by check or money order.

Chapter 9
Online Tools to Make It Easy

The part of the online auction process that more people find difficult than any other is learning to use FTP to get their photos uploaded to a server where potential bidders can access them. Guess what! You don't have to learn FTP or even have the software loaded on your computer!

A very useful tool available to dealers with Internet access is AuctionWatch.com (*http://www.auctionwatch.com*). One of the many features of the AuctionWatch.com site is that they provide, free of charge, 20,000K of space on their server to each member (registration is also free) and an automatic upload feature that makes this process unbelievably easy.

Here's how it works. Go to the AuctionWatch.com site and click on the "Message Center" link. There you should find another link to register (or, as a shortcut, simply go directly to (*http://www.auctionwatch.com/register.htm*). The only required information to register on AuctionWatch.com is your name and e-mail address. There are other questions on the registration form, but you needn't fill them out if you are concerned about privacy. Other than that, you must pick a screen name and password just as you have to do to register with any online auction. As always, remember your password or you won't be able to access the features of the site.

Once your registration is confirmed, you can begin using the free image hosting feature. From the AuctionWatch.com home page, click on the "image hosting and smart counters" link. You'll be taken to a screen where you can type your account name and password to enter. Once in, you will have the ability to browse your hard disk for the photos you want to upload (if you can't see the browse button, you don't have the latest version of Internet Explorer or Netscape and can link directly to the newest versions from here). When you click a browse button, a "Choose File" window will open allowing you to navigate through your hard disk until you find the photo you need. Select the correct photo and click "Open"—the file name will appear in the upload window of your browser.

You can upload three photos at a time, and each must be less than 400K in size. This is quite generous, and I don't recommend you EVER run photos of that size on online auctions—they simply take too long to load. Prospective bidders will tire of waiting and leave your auction,

http://www.auctionwatch.com

AuctionWatch.com

the definitive resource for the online auction community

Links

- Web Sites
- Image Hosting & Smart Counters
- Auction Postcards
- The Buzz
- Message Center
- Search
- About AuctionWatch.com
- Jobs @ AuctionWatch.com
- Contact Us

The Buzz

AuctionWatch.com Secures $9.6 Million in Series B Financing [AW]

Click for more articles

Auction Sites

[Search]

- Antiques (51)
- Art (9)
- Automobiles (11)
- Aviation (1)
- Bankruptcy (2)
- Boats (3)
- Books (2)
- Business to Business (9)
- Business Liquidation (4)
- Cameras (1)
- Charity (6)
- Clothing (4)
- Collectible Directories (7)
- Comics (4)
- Computers (29)
- Electronics (5)
- Ephemera (1)
- Estate (3)
- Firearms (8)
- Galleries (3)
- General

Auction Related Sites

The AuctionWatch.com list of auction related sites provides guaranteed links and descriptions for over 300 different sites. Our link-verifying spider crawls the links in our database every day to ensure that our links are current. From antiques to wine, the AuctionWatch.com list classifies both general and focused specialty auction sites in a concise and easy to navigate layout. Visit the **auction-related web sites section** or **browse the categories on the left side of this screen** to find the sites that meet your needs.

Free Image Hosting & New **Smart Counters- Millions of 'em Served Daily!**

Command higher selling prices and liven up your item's description with AuctionWatch.com's image hosting and smart counter system. It's the fast, free and easy way to add an image or counter to your auction item- there's no need to know complex codes, ftp programs or html. Best of all, it's free. Visit the **image hosting & smart counter section today!**

The Buzz - Auction Related News Updated Daily

The Buzz contains links to dozens of interesting articles on auctions. Whether you're an online auction buyer, seller, investor or just learning about auction trends, it's a great resource for auction specific happenings.

AuctionWatch.com's Message Center

AuctionWatch.com's Message Center has become the premier forum to discuss anything related to online auctions. It's a great place for seasoned veterans to discuss their auction experiences and for newbies to get the tips they need to do business safely and efficiently online. Easy to read and navigate, it's simply the best way to keep in touch with other auction participants. Want to see what the press has been raving about? **Stop by and speak your mind!**

IE eBay Quickscript* --> Windows 95/98, Internet Explorer Only!

The Internet Explorer eBay quickscript for windows 95/98 version 3.0 or higher is now available for download. This simple script allows you to type the word "find" in your browsers address bar, followed by the items you're searching for. The quickest way to search eBay!

To Install, **download the script here.** When prompted, select open it. You'll get confirmation that your windows registry has costing you bids and higher prices. Try keeping your files to 60K or less (see Chapter 11—Digital Strategies). Once you have one, two, or three files displayed in the upload windows, simply click the "Upload These Images" button. Your files will be transmitted and stored on the AuctionWatch.com server, and you will get a message telling you the upload was successful. The photo(s), along with their filenames, will display. If you scroll down this screen you will see that AuctionWatch.com even lists previous photos you have uploaded and keeps track of how much space you are using, as well as how much space you have available for more photos.

The next step is to select the photo(s) you want to use in your auction. Simply click on the empty box in the select column beside the filename of the photo(s) you want. Next, click on the "Attach to Auction" button and you will be prompted to designate which auction site you are using (eBay™, Amazon, or "other site" are the only selections), whether this is a new or existing auction, and if you want a counter added to your auction. Make the appropriate selections and then click on the "Add images/counter" button. The next screen you see will look just like the actual listing form used by the auction you have selected. You simply fill in the required fields just as you do when you list or update an item without using AuctionWatch.com, review your listing, and post it. Believe me, it's even easier than what you just read makes it sound!

One more thing you should be aware of when you use any public site like this—as more people begin to use it, server access typically slows down and your photo may load a bit slower for potential bidders than if you were using your ISP's server. However, if you follow the strategies outlined in this book and keep your photos to a minimum size, you will get acceptable performance from AuctionWatch.com. Or if you prefer to FTP files to your ISP's server, learn how in my companion book *The ABCs of Collecting Online*.

Price Guides

Online price guides are an area I expect to see really take off over the next two years, and who else but the Kovels would be one of the first on the scene with a general online price guide? As one of the leaders in publishing price guides and information for dealers and collectors, they have the experience and the trust to become one of the front-runners in this new area of Internet commerce.

By the time you have this book in your hands it might be old news, but as I'm writing this the Kovels Online Price Guide is brand new and offering free trial memberships. There is extensive information stored on this site, still in beta testing at this time. A search engine makes navigating through the 750+ categories and 150,000+ entries feasible—use it to locate items much as you would use the index of a book. Suggestions for improvement are being solicited from trial members, and the site will likely see some changes over the next few months as it strives to find the right value added formula to attract dealers and collectors.

Point your browser to *http://www.tias.com/stores/kovels/* and begin exploring. Browsing the categories is free, and the trial membership offers 50 peeks at prices for individual items. Once the site is established, it is almost certain that a yearly fee will apply for pricing information.

Antique Trader also has a general online price guide available now. Their online price guide contains all of the information contained in the 1995-1999 annual paperback editions, and unlimited access is available for $15.95 per year. Alternately, you can purchase the 1999 paperback price guide and get free access to the online version through 1999, also for $15.95. Sign up for either of these deals at *http://www.csmonline.com/priceguide*.

A good price guide for Victorian furniture and a few other miscellaneous categories is available at *http://www.slawinski.com*. Slawinski is an auction company that is posting actual auction results on their Web site in the form of a price guide. This is not only a creative form of advertising, but could eventually lead to an invaluable source of price information available at your fingertips if other auctioneers see value in it.

Art*fact* (*http://www.artfact.com*) is a subscription based online price guide available to art and antiques professionals. ArtFact Incorporated was founded in 1989 with the charter of providing the highest quality independent public auction information to serious professionals within the art and antiques world. The database, comprised of art, antiques, collectibles, and jewelry, has grown to over four million entries, and many of the most prestigious auction houses in the world contribute the information.

There are several good online price guides for specialized categories. If you're into diecast cars like Hot Wheels or Johnny Lightning, visit *http://www.alleyguide.com* for an extensive price guide of these items. There is also a Beanie Baby price guide on this site. Pez lovers can find a great site and price guide at *http://www.pezheads.com*. Fans of the

http://www.tias.com/stores/kovels/

KOVELS' on-line
PRICE GUIDE TO ANTIQUES & COLLECTIBLES

| Help | Home | Newsletter | Books | Leaflets | Videos | Stories and Articles |

Sign up for a FREE account today!
Registered Users Click Here!

KOVELS'
buy/sell/match

Welcome to KOVELS' ONLINE ANTIQUES & COLLECTIBLES PRICE GUIDE--The Internet antiques & collectibles reference site you can trust. At YOUR request we have compiled the information from five Kovels' price lists--more than **250,000 PRICES, FACTORY NAMES, DATES, and HISTORICAL TIDBITS**--into a fully searchable, cross-referenced, fun-to-browse database. Our Web site not only helps you establish values for unusual items, like a Federzeichnung vase, it shows you five-year market trends for mass-produced items, like an Adam Depression glass plate or a Roseville Magnolia vase.

With the glut of antiques information showing up on the Internet, why should you believe the prices listed here are accurate? We, RALPH and TERRY KOVEL, are collectors JUST LIKE YOU. We are also the best-read writers in the world of antiques and collectibles. We started years ago. The annual Kovels' Antiques & Collectibles Price List is written from scratch every year. We report actual prices in the marketplace. And, unlike others, the KOVEL name means we are the authors-every price and description has been reviewed for accuracy. We correct or delete thousands of errors.

There's more! We have written more than 90 publications for collectors ranging from handy take-with-you leaflets to comprehensive price guides to full-color reference books. We also publish an award-winning monthly newsletter, Kovels on Antiques and Collectibles, a monthly column in House Beautiful magazine, and a nationally syndicated weekly newspaper column.

But enough about us. To get started, REGISTER--IT'S FREE. Just fill out our simple questionnaire and you're on

T o search for a price, type the name of the item into the box below and click on the "What's it worth?" button.

Match All words.

Click HERE to browse the huge list of categories in our *Kovels' Online Antiques & Collectibles Price List.*

click here to enter

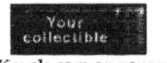
Put Kovels.com on your web site. Click here to find out how.

89

http://www.csmonline.com/priceguide.

Home | Buy/Sell | Online Price Guides | Reference | Forums | Collect.com Network

Price Guide   Search [   ]   Site Navigation

Antiques
Beans
Sports Collectibles

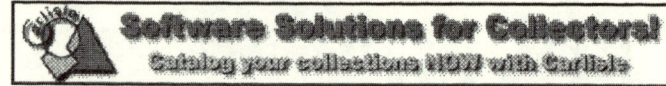

Welcome to the Online Price Guide section of Collect.com! With a huge number of items priced in thousands of categories, you will be sure to find the prices you are looking for! Please choose from any of the following options:

Antiques & Collectibles
Antique Trader's Annual Price Guide Database (1995-1999)
- Direct Online Purchase for 1 year- $15.95
- Purchase Book and Receive Free Access through 1999 - $15.95
- Register your Activation Card from the Antique Trader 1999 Annual Price Guide Book. Register Here
- View a sample from the Online Price Guide
- Registered Users click here to **Enter the Online Price Guide**
- Forget your User Name / Password? Click Here

Bean Bag Toys
Beans! Magazine Online Price Guide
- FREE access for all users

Sports Trading Cards & Memorabilia
Tuff Stuff Online Price Guide
- FREE access with online registration

The right to download and store or output the articles in Collect.com is granted to users for their personal use only. Any other reproduction, by any means - mechanical or electronic - without the express written permission of Collect.com is strictly prohibited.

© Copyright 1999 - Collect.com (TM) All rights reserved.

http://www.slawinski.com

HOME

MAP & LODGING

1999 AUCTIONS

HOW TO BUY

HOW TO SELL

ABOUT US

TERMS

ONLINE PRICE GUIDE

SLAWINSKI AUCTION COMPANY

August 1st Estates Auction

June 27th Estates Auction   *RESULTS*

May 31st, 1999 Estates Auction   *RESULTS*

6192 Hwy 9, Felton CA 95018 (831) 335-9000
antiques@slawinski.com

visitors since February 1997:

http://www.artfact.com

LINKS   SEARCH   HELP   HOME

ARTFACT OVERVIEW   CONTACT ARTFACT

Welcome to Art*fact*

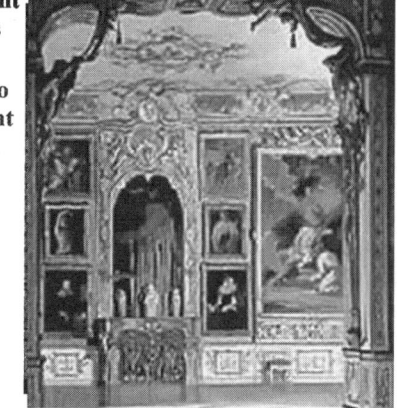

The World's largest complete and independent online resource of art, antiques, collectibles and jewelry auction sales records.

More than just a price guide, the Art*fact* Pro Internet is a professional research instrument with over 4 million unedited public auction sales results compiled from hundreds of participating auction houses worldwide. Determining market value and learning important information about an artist or manufacturer is only seconds away with Art*fact*.

Get the *facts* before you buy or sell with Art*fact*.

ArtFact, Incorporated 1130 Ten Rod Road - Suite E 104 North Kingstown, Rhode Island 02852
email sales@artfact.com 1-800-ARTFACT (278-3228)

http://www.ebay.com

home | my eBay | site map

Browse | Sell | Services | Search | Help | Community
find items | find members | personal shopper

165 items found for the search ""flue cover." Showing items 1 to 50.

"flue cover" [Go!]

Results by: THUNDERSTONE

e.g. "brown bear" -teddy more tips

Sort by: [Ending Date] ⊙ ascending ○ descending Search Active Items

Search Result
Completed Auctions
11:58:14 PDT

Item#	Item	Price	Bids	Ends
131666157	VICTORIAN FLUE COVER CARNATIONS C. KLEIN	$40.00	4	07/21 14:38
131668098	Unique Victorian Flue Cover w/Egyptian Scene	$29.01	9	07/21 14:40
131671282	VICTORIAN FLUE COVER TWO CHILDREN MINT	$165.00	22	07/21 14:50
131770848	Unique Victorian Lady Flue Cover (NEW)	$3.00	0	07/21 17:58
131776568	Beautiful Angel Girls Flue Cover (NEW)	$3.00	0	07/21 18:06
131776849	Spectacular Cherub Flue Cover (NEW)	$3.00	1	07/21 18:06
131776783	Noah's Ark Flue Cover (NEW)	$3.00	1	07/21 18:06
131776580	Adorable Boy On Dock Fishing Flue Cover (NEW)	$3.00	0	07/21 18:06
131847604	GERMAN FLUE COVER	$86.00	14	07/21 19:38
130460770	Black Memorabilia: Flue Cover	$215.00	15	07/21 22:57
131992547	Chimney flue cover picture	$78.01	11	07/22 06:54
132199948	Victorian Reverse Painting and/or Flue Cover	$11.50	2	07/22 16:11
130851043	Old, Vintage ,Poor Man's Flue Cover L@@k	$9.95	0	07/22 19:56
132480940	Vic. Flue Cover Boy & Girl "The Manuscript"	$104.09	10	07/23 07:31
132582692	VICTORIAN FLUE COVER ROSES BEES DELONGPRE	$164.05	20	07/23 12:49
132590815	VICTORIAN FLUE COVER SWEET LITTLE GIRL	$95.50	10	07/23 13:11

Gene® doll have a price guide for the dolls that are sold on the secondary market at *http://www.hobbyhouse.com*. All of the aforementioned price guides are available free of charge—there is a one-time fee of $25.00 for unlimited access to a Care Bears price guide found at *http://www.carebearjake.com*.

You can try to locate a price guide for your area of interest by using any of the search engines available on the Internet. If you aren't familiar with using search engines, they are explained in detail in my companion book ***The ABCs of Collecting Online***.

You can also use eBay™ as a reliable source for auction value of items. With over two million items up for sale at any given time, and an option to run a search among auctions completed in the past 30 days, you in essence have an extensive database of information for prices realized.

Go to *http://www.ebay.com* and click on the Search box at the top of the page. Once on the search page, scroll to the bottom where you will find an option to search completed auctions. Type a keyword or two into the box and your instant electronic price guide appears before your eyes.

Let's say you came across a nice flue cover at your local flea market that the seller thought was just a print in a metal frame and priced it at $8.00 (yes, this did happen to me very recently). You knew enough to buy it, but didn't have a good idea of value.

Using the eBay™ completed auction feature, I ran a search using the keywords "flue cover" and 165 items appeared that I could peruse at my convenience to look for examples similar to mine, complete with final auction values. While you may not find an exact match for your item, especially if it's not a mass produced collectible, you can get a pretty good feel as to what you should expect to receive as fair market value. And if you *are* dealing in mass marketed collectibles, you may well come up with many listings giving prices for the exact item you have. You might be surprised at how often the prices realized for identical items are within a few dollars of each other. Instant fair market value!

New sites are springing up to offer free photo posting services and other tools, one of which is auctionSpy (*http://www.auctionspy.net*). Not only does auctionSpy offer free counters and image hosting both in one location, they also have a unique feature called ClickBid™. ClickBid™ will list all of your auctions (both as a seller and a bidder) on your home page and allows you to place a bid on any of the items with one click of the mouse. In addition, if you use Microsoft Internet Explorer, you can download extension software that allows you to highlight an item num-

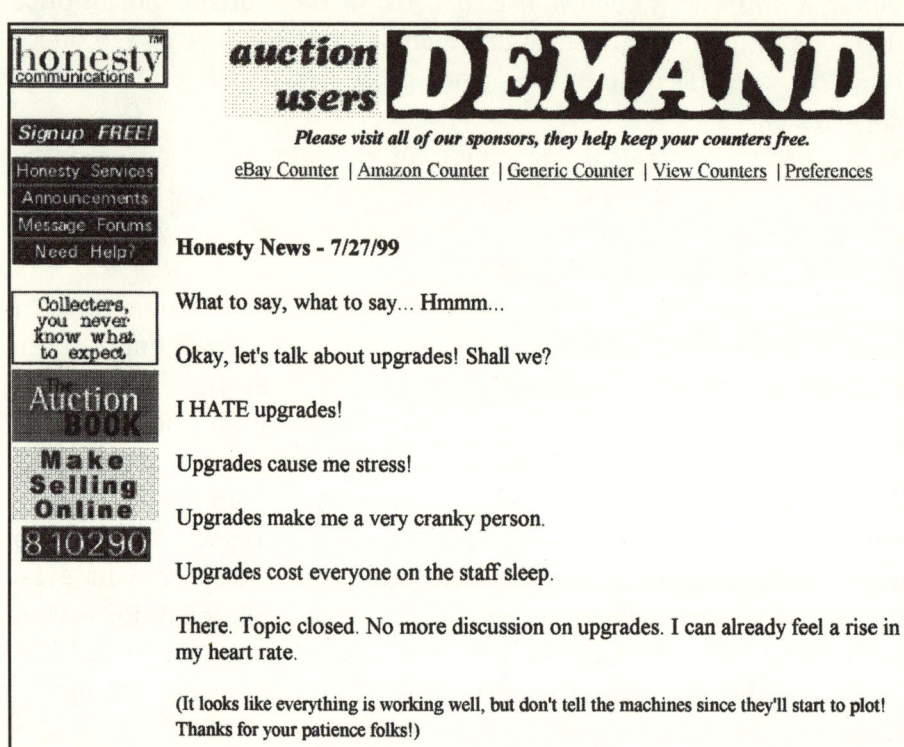

ber from an eBay search menu, right click, and place a bid on that item without ever visiting the actual listing! Be careful though-you are not given the opportunity to specify the bid amount-the program will simply place your bid at the next highest increment. As soon as you click the bid is placed so don't bid unless you mean it!

auctionSpy is also working on a feature that will show a list of all of your auctions regardless of which major auction site you are using, with an icon next to each entry to identify the auction. This will be a major asset to the users who want to use multiple auction sites but have steered away from doing so because of the hassle it requires to keep track of everything.

Counters

When you use your own ISP to host your auction photos but still want a counter keeping track of your page *hits,* point your browser to *http://www.honesty.com.* Here you can register and easily attach a count-

http://www.beseen.com

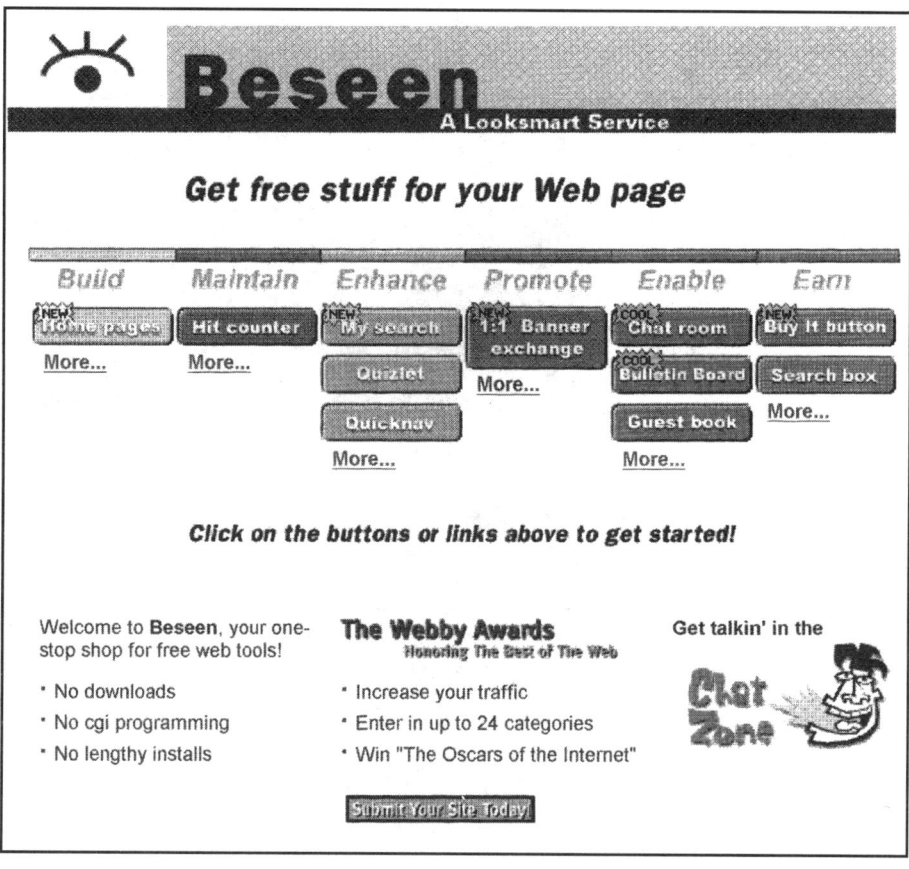

er to your eBay™, Amazon.com, or other auction—even your personal home page! The counters come in a wide variety of styles, and there is a statistical chart you can view on each counter that shows you what days and times your counter is registering the most visitors. All of this service is absolutely free—paid for by the advertising you will see on the site.

I have asked many dealers what they use the counters for—what type of information they glean from using one. The most common answer is, in the case of online auctions, that it helps them identify what items are hot and which ones are not. I personally would rather gauge how "hot" an item is from the number of bids it receives and the final auction value, but nonetheless this seems to be a valid reason for many to have a counter on their auction pages. If you're a statistics buff and believe that numbers don't lie, the statistical data now being offered by Honesty.com may allow you to identify peak bidding times and therefore give you an indicator of the best times to start and end your auctions.

There are other good reasons for using a counter. If you decide to delve into the HTML chapter of this book and build your own Web storefront, put a counter on it to track the number of visitors. If you don't want the number to be accessible to everybody use a *blind counter,* which can be set up to display your company logo in place of the counter, or to display nothing at all. Keep records of daily and weekly hits so that you have a database of information to review if you should decide to advertise your site. Hopefully your advertising will result in increased sales, but counters give you another way to assess the return on investment of your advertising dollars. They can help you refine your ad campaign to just the sources that seem to bring the best results.

Honesty.com has evolved from humble beginnings to offer more and better services every few months, and I'm sure they will continue in that vein. Tuck this site away in your Favorites folder and visit regularly to keep up with the coming auction tools they will be sure to offer in the near future.

A free counter site already offering some other Web tools is *http://www.beseen.com.* Although the auction counters must be cut and pasted into your auction listing, whereas with Honesty.com it is automatic for eBay™ and Amazon.com auctions, here you can build your own home page and add a personalized search engine to your site. You can add a feature to your Web site to survey your site visitors, and is a way to more easily navigate your site. All of this is free for the asking, just by joining Beseen.com.

PC Troubleshooting

Yes, if you know where to look, you can even find free help in troubleshooting your PC problems. A group of volunteers who try, and usually succeed, in helping you through computer related problems can be found at *http://tsinc.simplenet.com/index.hts*. Here you can search a database of previous problems and their solutions, and if you don't find your particular problem you can ask for help. The help form will ask some simple questions such as your computer experience level and give you the opportunity to explain your problem. In some cases you will receive more than one reply, giving you several options to try. When you find one that works, you should report back how the problem was fixed so that it can be added to the database.

http://www.mapquest.com

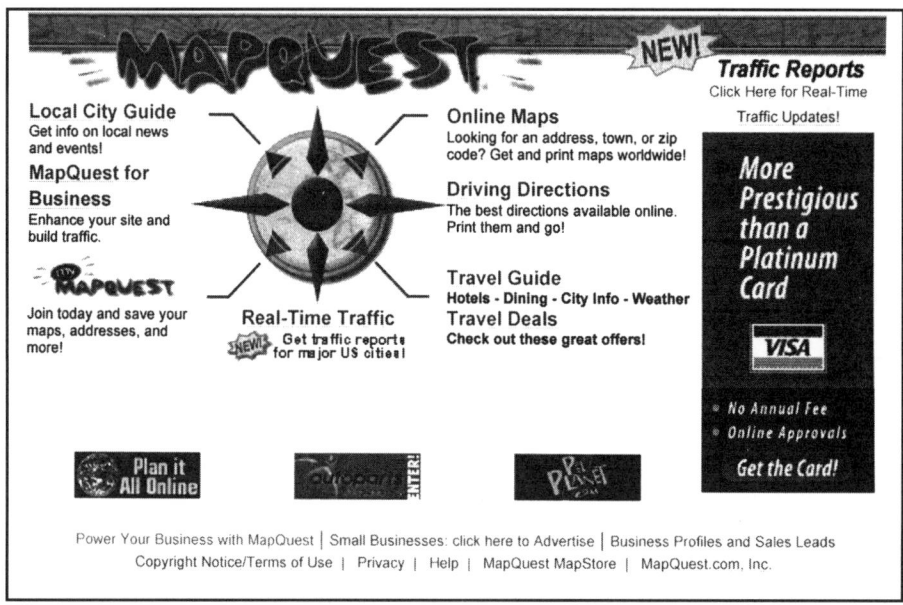

Finding Your Way

As I've told you, the Internet is much more than auction sites and malls. If you've ever heard the expression "if you can dream it, you can do it" the Internet proves that in many cases that statement is true. You can even find directions to that big auction you want to attend in a town several hours away with the click of a mouse.

Mapquest (*http://www.mapquest.com*) gives you the ability to type in the names of two different towns and not only get driving directions between the two, but total miles and the estimated drive time. Directions are supplied in either map form, or a "printer-friendly" format that you can print out and take with you. The site also offers a travel guide, travel deals, and a local city guide.

American Automobile Association (*http://www.aaa.com*) also offers driving directions online, but you must be a member to access them. If you are an AAA member you can also order a TripTik® or maps online and have them delivered to your home.

Pack and Ship

I'm partial to the United States Postal Service. They offer dependable service at reasonable prices and throw in free supplies to boot! If you haven't taken advantage of their online services, visit *http://www.usps.gov* and get with the program! While they can't weigh your package for you (at least at the Web site they can't—visit your local post office and they'll be happy to), they do supply a rate calculator that will give you an accurate shipping cost for anything from priority mail to parcel post to oversized packages. You can track express mail, and confirm delivery for priority mail and parcel post. There is also a zip code locator that identifies zip codes with towns, and another tool that gives you the zip+4 code for any address.

Oh, I mentioned free supplies, didn't I? By visiting *http://supplies.usps.gov* you can take advantage of free boxes, tape, labels, and other goodies that will make it much easier to fulfill your shipping responsibilities. While most local post office branches carry a selection of the more commonly used boxes, the Web site will give you a list of many other available materials. You can also call 1-800-222-1811 to order post office supplies.

There is now a tool on eBay™ that allows potential bidders to calculate their shipping costs without even contacting you! Through an agreement with Mailboxes Etc. and iShip.com, you can add a link to your auction listings that will calculate shipping costs from your zip code to the zip code of your prospective buyer. The process happens when you are listing your item, and can be accessed from a link on the eBay™ Sell Your Item page.

Clicking on the link brings you to a form you where you input the following information: 1) Select the carriers you are willing to use. The choices are the United States Postal Service, Federal Express, United Parcel Service, and Airborne Express. 2) Select your pickup/drop off option. You can choose from taking the package to a drop box, taking it to a branch office of your carrier, having a scheduled pickup at your location or calling for an immediate pickup at your location. 3) Enter the zip code from where the package will be shipped. 4) Enter the weight of the package. You must also supply dimensions if the package is oversized. 5) Specify the amount of insurance on the package, if any. 6) Specify the amount of handling charges you wish to add, if any. You can specify handling charges as a percentage of the shipping charges or a fixed amount. You then preview what the bidder will see, and you can even plug in a zip code and have it calculate shipping charges on the information you have just entered if you want to double check the amounts being displayed to bidders. You then click on a button that creates the HTML for your link, which you then copy and paste into your item description.

When a buyer clicks on the link in your description, they need only specify their zip code, whether they are a business or a residence, and if they need a guaranteed delivery time. A chart is then displayed showing the shipping amount for this particular package, with a breakdown by the different carriers the seller has specified. This effectively solves a problem that has plagued buyers since the inception of online auctions—wondering what shipping will cost. While it adds an extra minute or two to the listing process, the value added is enormous and I expect this type of information to become as important as having a photo with your listing.

eBay a-go-go™

If you've really become an eBay™ junkie and can't wait to find out when you've been outbid on an item, win an auction, or sell something, SkyTel has the program for you. eBay a-go-go™ notifies you via wireless pager when any of these three events occurs, as well as providing a regular dose of eBay™ news.

Along with a one-time $20 activation charge, for $55 you purchase 2000 message units and receive a unique eBay™ pager. Each auction notification, on average, expends four of those message units, which means your initial purchase nets you roughly 500 auction notifications. The notification itself is a condensed version of the message you receive via your computer e-mail, and you continue to receive those messages on your computer. There are no contracts to sign and everything is paid up front, but the message units must be used within six months of the time you receive your pager. Additional message units can then be purchased on a sliding scale cost.

This unit also functions as a regular pager that friends, family, and business associates can use to contact you. For complete details on this program as well as available add-on options like voice mail and caller ID, go to *http://www.skytel.com/ebay*.

If you have a current wireless device that has an e-mail address and accepts alphanumeric messaging, you can sign up for the basic service and use your existing device. You will not receive the eBay™ news broadcasts or be able to access your messages via telephone as you can with the SkyTel service.

Site Maps

Let's not forget about the auction sites themselves, and the wealth of online help they make available. The easiest way to get an overview of what is available on any major auction is to visit their *site map* (some refer to it as a *site guide*). A site map is simply a page that lists a brief explanation of all of the options available to the visitor as well as a link to get to that part of the site easily. eBay™ provides a help section on their site map, with links to bulletin boards where users can ask for assistance, guides for both buyers and sellers, direct support for new users, even an images/HTML board for assistance in those areas. The boards are part of what make eBay™ a community—many users monitor the boards and offer useful advice to others seeking assistance.

Chapter 10
Auction Enhancing Software

As is the case with most successful new business opportunities, other smaller businesses have evolved that cater to the "specialized needs" that invariably arise when something of the size and scope of online auctions becomes popular. Software has been developed that will jazz up the look of your auction listing, make volume listing easier, keep records, and even automatically bid for you if you can't be at the computer when a "must-have" item is closing.

I made it a point earlier to make sure you understand that selling on the Internet can be deceivingly time consuming. You may have noticed in the chapter of stories from successful sellers that the ones who are listing hundreds of items daily, or even weekly, use specially designed software and have employees other than themselves. In this chapter we will look at some of the software available for purchase and the benefits it brings to your business. At this point in time, nearly all of the software being developed is streamlined to work only for eBay™ in a Microsoft Windows 95/98 environment, with these two companies being the major players in their respective marketplaces.

Merlin (http://www.pctechzone.com/merlin)

Merlin ($12.95) comes from veteran eBay™ user Jason Novak of Rice Lake, Wisconsin. It is an exceptional compilation of many individual programs that are the essence of what experienced eBay™ traders are looking for. While many online auction software packages utilize HTML, Javascript, or Java language, which works with your computer but isn't native language, Merlin uses only true 32-bit Windows 95 executable files in its makeup. The differences are obvious and truly beneficial to the user.

First let's look at updates to the software, an issue that any veteran computer user will tell you is every bit as annoying as your hardware being obsolete six months after you buy it. Many software programs, particularly anti-virus types, need to be updated every few months, costing the end user additional money each time. With Merlin, subsequent updates are free, and to make it easier yet, each time you launch the Merlin software it automatically connects to its home server to check if there is an update to download.

http://www.pctechzone.com/merlin

Merlin
"Your Personal Auction Wizard"

options

news

current ad

ordering

links

faq

contact me

bulkLister

downloads

owners only

Merlin Full Install
v5.7 (4.3 megs)

Merlin Upgrade
5.3c > v5.7 (470K)

bulkLister Lite Full Install
v2.1b (4.7 megs)

bulkLister Lite Upgrade
v2.0 > 2.1b (275k)

free to public

Merlin AdultSearch
v1.2b (2.2 megs)

AdultSearch Upgrade
v1.1 > v1.2b (55K)

Welcome to the world of Merlin

Merlin is the most powerful auction management software today with a wide variety of tools to aid both eBay buyers and sellers. Created by a very active eBay user it features automatic bidding (or sniping), end-of-auction reminders, auction listers, feedback searches, and much more packaged in an innovative and easy to use interface. Check out my current ad for a complete description.

For those of you who've come looking for the eBay PowerUser Tools suite, you're at the right place. The name was changed to better fit the new program layout.

Latest News

Merlin v5.7 ... IA Fixes and New Dialer Routines
August 7 - 9:07pm

A few more "IA" fixes to AfterAuction and to the category refresh buttons ... improved the dialer routines by removing the "Online" and "Offline" buttons and letting the computer figure it out ... it now checks for other snipe auctions ending soon before disconnecting, and pops up a windows for 60 seconds asking if it should hang up just incase you don't want it to.

AdultSearch v1.2b ... New "IA" Fixes
July 29 - 3:01pm

eBay has unveiled it's Information Architecture, or IA. Basically they tweaks some pages and added a more complex navigation system on the tops of their pages. It also affected AdultSearch, I'm checking Merlin & others, but so far only Retriever may have been affected. Don't know if they're ever going to go back to the interface they released for about a day until eBay crashed.

Merlin v5.3d .... New Dialer Script/AfterAuction Search
July 23 - 10:22pm

Support, another issue near and dear to many users, is available in the form of a 70+ page manual (in HTML format for easy browsing) with screenshots and tutorials included. Jason, the creator of Merlin, also offers technical support via e-mail or ICQ to answer any questions you might have.

In the early days of Merlin, the software was shipped on disk. It has evolved in both programs and features to the point that it now ships on CD-ROM even though there is plenty of room on the CD after the software is copied. Rather than waste this space, nearly 7000 images have been included, such as 500+ animated GIF files, that you can use to spice up your auctions.

Now for the tools themselves. I'll examine each one individually and let you assess the benefits to your particular situation.

Snipe: Snipers are a way of life on eBay™. Some of the online auctions utilize *dynamic auction closing*, where the auction is extended a specified number of minutes whenever a new bid is placed. Although they are considering making dynamic close an option, for now on eBay™ when it's done, it's done, leaving the door open for somebody to place a bid with a few seconds left and knock you out of high bidder position. There are only two ways to combat this strategy-one is to sit at your computer to monitor the auction when it ends. The other is to utilize a snipe program, and become a sniper yourself.

Snipe allows you to specify maximum bid amounts for as many auctions as your computer memory can hold. When the time comes for an auction to end, snipe will dial in to your Internet connection if you're not already online, connect to the ending auction and place a last-minute bid for you. Snipe will only bid up to a maximum you specify, and eBay™ will record only the minimum amount needed to win the auction. While few things in life are guaranteed, your chances of winning auctions increase dramatically when using snipe.

AfterAuction: If you're a bulk seller this tool is particularly useful in managing the tasks that need to be done when the show is over. AfterAuction searches for users you have not left feedback for, and interfaces with the feedback tool so you can easily rectify that situation. It can also search for users who haven't left feedback for you, useful if you're a new user trying to build a respectable feedback file. You can run searches on all auctions, auctions by a specific user, or specific auctions by item number. AfterAuction also interfaces with the e-mail tool, allowing you to send bulk e-mail messages using predefined templates, such as letting multiple users know you've left them feedback.

Seller: Seller helps you keep track of your eBay™ customers. It stores their personal information-names and addresses-as well as the auctions they bid on. There are also six customizable "flags" that you can tailor to your record keeping system. For instance, you can designate a "when paid" flag, and check it when payment is received..

A section for "Other Expenses" provides six more customizable flags for each auction. You can take advantage of this feature to keep records on things like eBay™ fees and shipping fees. By keeping the right information, you can then print a report for a specified time period detailing the sale price and associated fees, taking some of the wear and tear out of tax time. This report feature also allows you to create an e-mail list for all of your eBay™ customers.

Power Reminder: Even if you choose not to utilize all of the features of the snipe tool, you have another option to keep you in touch with ending auctions. Power Reminder constantly (while you're online) monitors the auctions you specify, making a cash register sound when a bid is placed on any of them. When an auction on your list is about to close, a dialog box pops up as your reminder, giving you plenty of time to monitor the auction or arm the snipe tool. And you have "Quick Buttons" that make it easy to add any auctions you have listed or bid on to your list. This is not just a buyer tool-adding your listings also allows you to keep track of how the bidding is progressing.

Power Feedback: Everybody likes to build his or her positive feedback stable, but giving feedback can be bothersome and time consuming. Power Feedback breaks down into six categories covering positive, neutral, and negative for both buyer and seller and provides a sample feedback message that you can customize in each category. You can also add your own feedback comments and store them, making them available for later use-and you can send multiple users the same feedback message together, a real time saver.

Bidder List: If you've ever had to contact everyone who bid on one of your auctions to inform them of revised information, or individually e-mailed everyone who bid in a Dutch Auction you ran, you'll appreciate this tool. Bidder List will compile an e-mail address list of everybody who has bid on an auction simply by entering the auction item number, and with one click will then open your e-mail program with those addresses already inserted, ready for you to type your message. Notifying Dutch Auction bidders was never this easy!

Shopper: Shopper works in much the same way as eBay™ Personal Shopper, with one distinct advantage—this one will search auction sites other than eBay™ if you instruct it to. Just load up some keywords, specify which auction sites you want it to search, and Shopper will return information on the item, auction server, and the URL for each one it finds. By double clicking on any entry, you are taken directly to that listing.

BulkLister Lite: Believe it or not, Merlin also contains a lite version of its bulk listing tool. Like other bulk listers reviewed in this chapter, bulkLister lite works with Mister-Lister, the bulk listing tool from eBay™. Built-in SMPT functionality allows you to send all of your compiled auctions without needing an external mail program, and a feature still in the testing stage scans your entries for blatant errors before you upload them. You also get a direct link to eBay's batch management page, allowing you to review your batch before submitting it. There is an "Add To Batch" option that allows you to move auctions from one batch to another, so you can control auctions that end at the same time. You don't have to be connected to the Internet while you create your auctions, saving you precious time online if you are using a metered service or allowing someone else to access the Internet connection while you prepare auctions.

The only difference between bulkLister lite and the full bulkLister tool, which is sold separately for $12.95, is that with the lite version you can load up only three auctions at a time for submission. With the full version that number increases to 100.

There are even more tools available, including a time saving search option and the ability to "blacklist" buyers or sellers that have wronged you in the past. If you really need to see more, visit the Web site, but I think you get the picture. This package is well worth the purchase price.

Blackthorne Software Auction Products (http://www.blackthornesw.com)

Blackthorne Software from Sayre, Pennsylvania has developed the definitive software package for listing and tracking your eBay™ auctions. AuctionAssistant is a well integrated group of three different programs consisting of AuctionAssistant2, which includes a great auction formatter called Ad Studio, AuctionTicker, for keeping track of your current auctions, and MegaSets, which gives you the ability to create auto-

http://www.blackthornesw.com

| Home | Feedback | Contents | Search | Top Page 1 |

Blackthorne Software

- News
- Products
- Ordering
- Support
- Download
- Links

Important info regarding the eBay change of format on 7/27/99.

eBay converted to their new IA architecture on 7/27/99. We have already prepared a version of AuctionAssistant that works with the new page formats. Please go to our downloads page to find out how to upgrade for the new format.

AuctionAssistant Pro is now in Beta Test!

We are very pleased to announce that AuctionAssistant Pro is in the second round of beta testing. For more information on the upcoming features, please visit the Coming Soon... page under Products.

Awards and Reviews

We've recently been rated 5 stars by the Super Shareware Library.

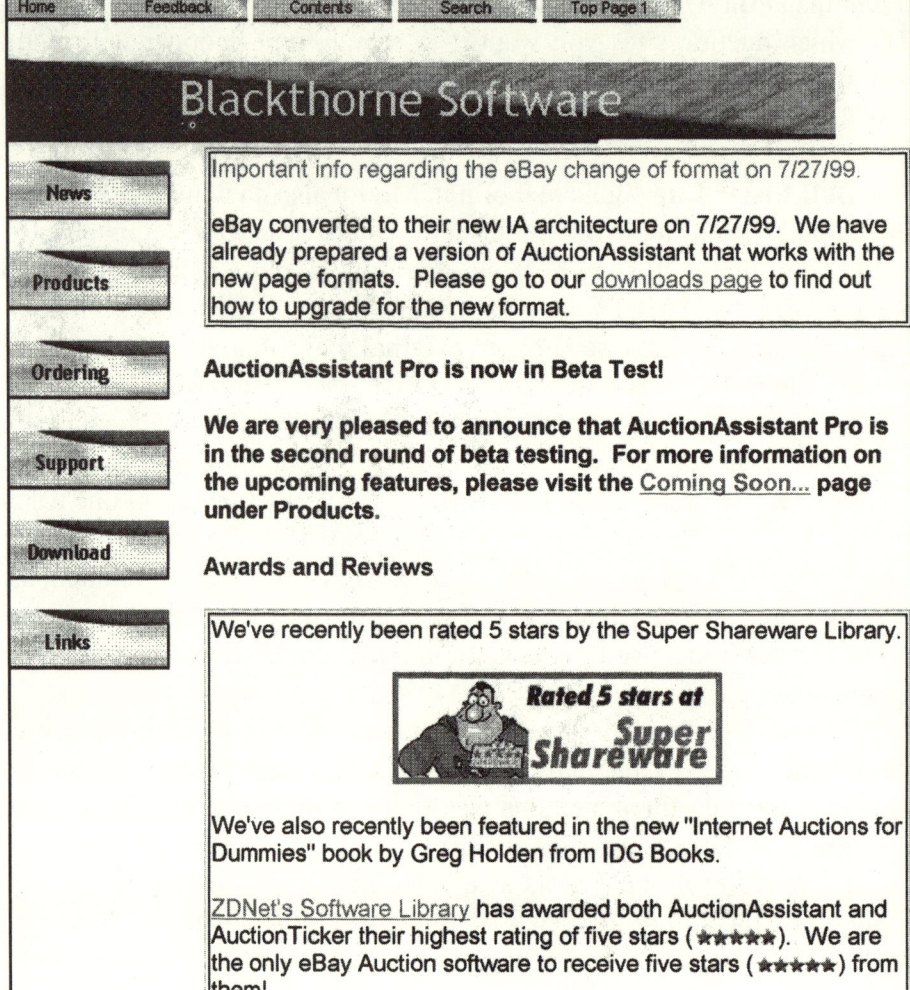

We've also recently been featured in the new "Internet Auctions for Dummies" book by Greg Holden from IDG Books.

ZDNet's Software Library has awarded both AuctionAssistant and AuctionTicker their highest rating of five stars (★★★★★). We are the only eBay Auction software to receive five stars (★★★★★) from them!

On 4/14 we were chosen as the Pick of the Day at DaveCentral. Click here to find out what they had to say about us.

You can also check out the recent review of Auction Assistant 2 in the Dave Report.

matic listings with selected themes. The three programs are sold separately, and AuctionAssistant2 and AuctionTicker can be used independently of each other, but all are designed to work as a group. Let's look at the features of each program individually.

AuctionAssistant2 ($59.95) is a well-designed control panel that allows you to enter your auction information, including up to three photos already stored on your computer. You can browse your hard disk for the photo you want, select it, and AuctionAssistant2 will display the correct file name and show you the actual photo(s) you have selected in a small browser window. You can then automatically upload the photo(s) to your server and post your auction to eBay™. AuctionAssistant2 then becomes a useful archival system that keeps an electronic paper trail to aid you in record keeping.

Another feature of AuctionAssistant2 is the Ad Studio, which allows you to change the colors of your type and backgrounds for your ads. Ad Studio also contains some preset "themes" that use pleasing color combinations and add music to your auctions. There are, including the default theme, a total of 20 different variations included with AuctionAssistant2 version 2.2. Two of the themes are Parchment, with an appropriate background and yellow or brown type, or Money, with dollar signs on a green background with white and black type. Most themes are accompanied by music—the music files are supplied with the software and easily uploaded to your server.

AuctionAssistant2 offers the following benefits to the PC-based eBay™ auction user:
- A complete database for maintaining and tracking your auctions.
- Automatic creation of beautifully formatted listings using Ad Studio (a subprogram of AuctionAssistant2) without the need to know any HTML.
- Automatic uploading of images to your server (up to three photos per auction), and the automatic inclusion of those images in your listings.
- Automatic fill-in of data on the eBay™ forms as well as your listing.
- Automatic retrieval of data from eBay's screens for storage in your database, reducing the amount of typing you must do.

AuctionTicker ($19.95) is an automated program that will log on to the Internet, search for the auction information you want to know about, and then log off. You don't even have to be in the room—your update will be waiting for you when you return. You can choose to have the information displayed in table form, as a scrolling stock-ticker-like form, or both. If you have a soundcard and speakers, you can program AuctionTicker to sound an "alarm" when an auction on your list is about to close (I use the sound of a cash register ringing to remind me it's time to check my bid and possibly bid again). It's a great way to keep from missing out on those must-have items!

Some of the most impressive features of AuctionAssistant2, when compared to other auction creation software I've looked at, is that it is virtually "preprogrammed" in many ways. All of the links to your eBay™ pages that are needed to keep track of your activity are embedded in the software—with other programs you must either know the URL of the various eBay™ pages or visit each one and copy and paste the URL from your browser address window. If in the future eBay™ does change the URLs of their pages, Blackthorne keeps a list of the new address links on their Web site, making it easy for you to update your software.

AuctionAssistant2 also allows you to browse your hard disk for your photos and automatically uploads them to your server. With other less expensive software you are required to remember the path to your photos and manually type it in—then upload as you normally would using FTP. I don't know about you, but I think having to know and remember the folders and subdirectories and file names of my photos without being able to browse for them is a pain!

In addition, AuctionAssistant2 allows you to easily preview and make changes to your auction. You can effectively toggle back and forth between the text panel and Ad Studio panel, making and testing changes at will. Other software copies your ad to your Windows clipboard and you then have to paste it into the eBay™ listing form. In short, AuctionAssistant2 not only gives you the best looking auctions, it saves you time. That is known in business as a WIN-WIN.

Here are the primary benefits associated with using AuctionTicker:
- Constantly displays a "stock-ticker-like" window (which is actually a scrolling banner), the eBayID, description, current price, high bidder, and ending date of the auctions you specify.
- Customizable—you choose which fields you want to view—or display the auctions in a table format.
- Information can be sorted by any column.

- Sounds an alarm when an auction on your list is about to close.
- Retrieves information on all auctions where you are a seller or bidder with one touch.
- Retrieves information only about auctions you specify in a custom list.
- At user defined intervals, AuctionTicker will log on to the Internet, download the latest auction information for the auctions you're interested in, and then log off, or leave you logged on if you prefer.
- Refreshes the ticker up to four times each day at times you specify, or every set amount of minutes.
- Updates the ticker at any time with the touch of a button.
- If you also own AuctionAssistant, the prices in your AA database will automatically be updated with each refresh of AuctionTicker.
- Click on any EbayID in the Table View, and that auction will be loaded into your browser.
- Click the print button to print the status of your current auctions, or you can set AuctionTicker to print the data for you after each refresh automatically.
- All times in AuctionTicker are local to you!
- Supports AOL users except for automatic connect/disconnect.
- Supports Proxy Server connections.
- Automatic recovery for connection and Internet problems (no dial tone, someone on the phone, busy signal, no response from Internet, etc.)

AuctionTicker also serves a useful purpose that it was not necessarily designed for—that of sending a "ping" to your ISP at time intervals you designate, keeping you from being disconnected during idle Internet time. This is accomplished by setting the ticker to refresh every 10 minutes (number of minutes is adjustable). While the program has the capability to automatically log you on and off when you're not connected to the Internet, if you are already connected it will find your information on eBay™ to update itself at the specified time intervals, effectively causing enough activity so that you don't get *booted*. Of course, this can also be accomplished with your e-mail program by setting it to check mail every 5-10 minutes and leaving in run in the background.

Some people will say you should not be connected to the Internet at all times, as you are using *bandwidth* that can add to Internet congestion.

I agree with this statement, and would hope that people who spend just a few minutes or even a few hours online each day would not get in the habit of staying connected. However, if you spend most of your time online and are frequently interrupted only to find you've been disconnected when you return, AuctionTicker can help.

MegaSet#1 ($19.95) and/or *MegaSet#2 ($19.95),* can add even more pizzazz to your auctions! While I usually don't recommend weighing your eBay™ pages down with a lot of bells and whistles, if you're inclined to do so MegaSets allows you to quickly design great ads with themesets like Patriotic, Pythonesque, or 2001 Space Odyssey. There are also holiday themesets for Valentines Day, Halloween, and Christmas. All are complete with backgrounds, colored type, and music, and the files are optimized to take up as little space as possible.

A themeset is a collection of ad themes. An ad theme is a collection of colors, fonts, animations, sounds and backgrounds all meant to convey a common feeling or idea. AuctionAssistant2 can apply ad themes to your listings to create the HTML for beautiful, interesting and entertaining listings. For instance, if you have a western item to sell, you may want to use the "Wild West" theme. This theme has a desert sand background with a dark brown table and yellow and white writing in an old west font, and you can even download *midi* files from the internet to play in the background. An animated image of a cowboy is shooting at the text description of your item.

If you are in the camp that believes a colorful, musical auction listing gets more attention and encourages bidding, MegaSets is for you. And if you don't want to use the music, or any of the other ad components, they are easily edited out of the final auction version.

AuctionPoster98™ (http://www.auctionposter.com)

The main challenge to AuctionAssistant2 at this point in time seems to be coming from a software package called AuctionPoster98™. The concept here is to pay as you go rather than buy the software outright.

AuctionPoster98™ uses a monetary system made famous by the New York Subway system—paying with tokens. You can download the software for free, and any upgrades released are free, but you must then buy posting privileges and/or purchase tokens to use it. For instance, image hosting is made available, as is hosting of music files, for roughly $.15 to $.40 per auction, depending on the amount of server space you con-

http://www.auctionposter.com

The World's Most Powerful Auction Posting Tool

| News | Download | Pricing | Support | Search |

With **AuctionPoster98**™ you will easily create auctions for eBay™ that look great and help you make more money. Our program is the easiest posting tool available for eBay! If you have any problems our support staff is there to help. AuctionPoster is a great tool to save you from losing valuable time during eBay outages.

At a glance **AuctionPoster98**™ will:

- Create all your HTML.
- Enter all of the default eBay™ fields for you saving you tons of time.
- Automatically upload your pictures to the ftp site of your choice, or use our **AuctionPictures**™ site for automated hosting features. If you know how to click a button you know how to add a picture to your auction! It's that easy.
-   Put a free counter in your auction by clicking just one button. No more cut and paste or going to web pages or any of that other hokey pokey crud!
-   Spell check your auctions with just a click with our built in spell checker.
- Allow you to save your auctions so that you can open them and click "Post" to post them again.
- Create all your auctions offline if you like, leaving your phone line free.
- Supports eBay's bulk listing mechanism via **Mister Lister**. Create great looking auctions and then have AuctionPoster send them all at once for you to eBay Up to 100 auctions at a time.
- Host your images on the **AuctionPictures**™ web site if you don't have FTP Space.
- Supports **all** ISP's. Support built in for major ISP's such as **AOL**, **Earthlink, Mindspring**, **Netcom, Prodigy, ATT Worldnet**, etc.

AuctionPoster98™ allows you to create auctions quickly without knowing any HTML. However, if you know HTML, it's even more powerful! Once an auction has been created and saved, you can open it and post it again at any time. **AuctionPoster98**™ runs under Windows 95, Windows 98, or Windows NT.

For more details and screenshots on **AuctionPoster98**™ click here.

AuctionPoster98™ is a trademark of AuctionPoster™.
All other products mentioned are registered trademarks or trademarks of their respective companies.
Questions or problems regarding this web site should be directed to WebMaster@AuctionPoster.com
Copyright © 1998-1999 AuctionPoster. All rights reserved.

AuctionPoster
PO Box 8131
Foster City, CA 94404-8131
TEL: (916) 780 - 0998

sume. Three tokens will buy you 250K of space, and additional 100K blocks can be had for one token each.

Tokens will cost you anywhere from five to 15 cents each, depending on the quantity you purchase—spend $10 for fifteen or you can splurge and pay $300 for 6,000 tokens to get the five cent rate, with varying rates in between. You also pay $6.95 per month to post your listings, or $29.95 for a one-year posting pass, again with variable rates in between. Once you purchase your posting pass, it does not include picture hosting—you still need tokens if you're not using your own ISP's server for free hosting.

Even though I didn't particularly care for the token system, I use my ISP's server to host my photos and therefore would need only a posting pass to utilize the software. By purchasing one-year passes, I could use AuctionPoster98™ for two years before it would cost as much as the purchase price of AuctionAssistant2. So I decided to test-drive the free download, which comes with 20 tokens to get you started.

The download comes zipped, so before you go anywhere you must have unzipping software on your computer and know how to use it. The most commonly used unzipping software is WinZip, and you can find it at (http://www.winzip.com).

After unzipping the program, I ran it for the first time and was immediately greeted with a message that it did not support the 640x480 resolution of my monitor. While many people still operate in this resolution, as a Web designer I know it's impossible to design for every type and size of monitor. The message does tell you to change to 800x600 resolution, and how to accomplish that. I didn't change my resolution and had no major problems using the software and seeing everything.

The control panel looks strikingly similar to AuctionAssistant2, and you fill in titles and descriptions in almost identical manners. However, AuctionAssistant2 gives you the ability to change the color of any block of type easily—AuctionPoster98™ does not. So while both give you the option of adding backgrounds, AuctionAssistant2 also allows you to change type color to customize your look to blend with those backgrounds.

Next I found out that if I wanted to use one of the AuctionPoster98 stylized counters, I needed to purchase it with tokens. No way this dealer is paying for counters, not with all of the free ones offered on the Internet (check out *http://www.honesty.com* for all the free counters you need). I guess for some people the convenience of being able to add a counter at the time you create the auction is worth a few pennies, but personally I'll do without counters or add the free ones after the auction is created rather than pay for them.

Once you have your title and description input, you must set a reserve price—the program will not accept a blank entry. For no reserve, you must still enter 0.00. Now check the correct boxes for who pays shipping, etc. and it's time to add a photo. You can browse for your photo just like you do with AuctionAssistant2, but when you add it to your auction another message tells you that your photo must be in an AuctionPoster98™ media directory. It then prompts you to copy your file to a place where it will be accessible. Unless you don't mind having two copies of each of your photos saved on your computer you will have to conform to the needs of this software when saving and storing your picture files.

If you choose to use your own ISP as your server for storing photos, you will also have to fill in some information so that the program knows how to use your FTP connection. If you're not FTP literate, this will be difficult and you should be near the phone to call your ISP and ask questions. Some of the information can be found by launching your current FTP program and clicking on Edit Session to view the settings that are already stored on your computer.

A feature of AuctionPoster98™ that I thought showed potential was the ability to select a day and time to actually post your auction—you could create several auctions and instruct the program to upload them later. Unfortunately, while at first this option appears to be active, it in fact is not available and I was instructed to send e-mail to a given address if I liked the idea! What's not to like? It's an option—if I don't like it I don't have to use it. Maybe this feature will actually be a reality in future versions.

When your information is where it belongs, you click on Post and are connected to the eBay™ page that you usually see after you have listed your auction and clicked review to proceed to the verification step. You then finish listing the item as you normally would if you were not using the software.

http://www.listerpro.com

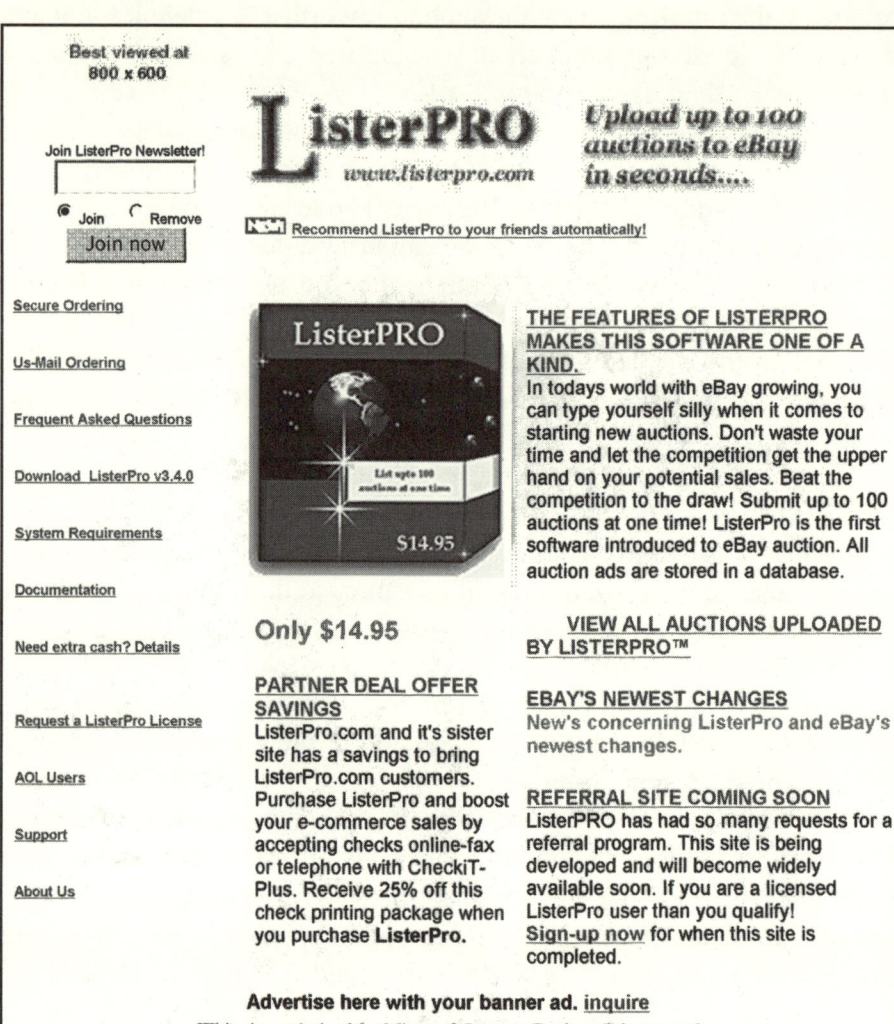

ListerPro (http://www.listerpro.com)

There are plenty of full-time eBay™ dealers who are more interested in listing hundreds of items daily without the emphasis on how fancy they look. To aid in that cause, *ListerPro ($14.95)* allows you to input your static information once and easily change the items (starting bids, reserves, descriptions, etc.) that need to be altered for individual listings. It then builds a database of your listings that you can access and change or update at any time, and finally allows you to upload and post up to 100 listings at a time to eBay™, utilizing eBay's Mister-Lister bulk listing tool. Mister-Lister is not designed for manual use, so make the small investment in ListerPro if you intend to do bulk listing on eBay™. You can find Mister-Lister instructions at *http://pages.ebay.com/aw/mr-lister.html*.

ListerPro is a useful tool and a time saver, but don't expect miracles. You must still take photos and write descriptions—two of the most time consuming activities associated with selling via Internet auctions. A good description and photo are mandatory for successful selling, and cannot simply be ignored. At this point in time there is no good way around the time commitment other than to hire an employee to do some of the work for you.

Since ListerPro works in conjunction with eBay™ and its Mister-Lister tool, when uploading your auctions you may experience slowness due to the enormous amount of users constantly using eBay™. However, every ListerPro user I have talked to agrees that it is still a real time saver over listing the auctions individually.

Another nuance of going through Mister-Lister is that all auctions uploaded from ListerPro in one batch have the same ending times. Some bulk listers like this feature, rather than have their auction end times spread out over a day or several days. However, if you are listing similar items that you think may attract the same bidder (i.e. several different items that together make up a set), you should upload them in different batches. Otherwise, if that bidder does find your listings and they are willing to watch your auctions end with the intent of bidding as high as they need to, they won't get that opportunity if everything ends at the same time.

Power Lister™ (http://www.powerlister.com)

A pay-as-you-go bulk loading program is also available for eBay™, with support for BoxLot, Up4Sale, and Haggle Online available now and Amazon.com Auctions and Yahoo! Auctions in the works. Power Lister™ allows you to post multiple auctions from one form and place then into a "holding bin" to be uploaded together. It is a convenience tool targeted toward helping sellers post their listings quickly. Up to 100 listings may be submitted simultaneously from one form. Single posts are also permitted using Power Lister forms. Repeated use of the form using up to 100 posts per form could generate hundreds of listings in a short time period.

After the initial form is filled in, the user has the option to review each listing individually for errors prior to the final submittal. Once the final submittal has been placed, the seller can resume the normal functions of the respective auction site. Therefore, the seller will receive confirmations and notices via e-mail from the auction site as if the listings were submitted at the auction site.

While registration is free, the fee to use Power Lister™ is 10 cents (US) per listing submitted to an auction via their Web site. The fee is independent of any other auction fees that may occur for placing items for sale at an auction site.

http://www.powerlister.com

POWER LISTER™
The Fastest Way to List Multiple Items in Auctions

AUCTIONS SUPPORTED
- eBay Auction
- eBay's Mister Lister™
- BoxLot Auction
- Haggle Online
- Up4Sale Auction *New!*

Power Lister is committed to providing the most convenient and fastest methods for posting items for sale to community auctions. You can post up to 100 items at once and up to 500 items a day to your favorite auction.

JOIN NOW! (Free Membership)

How It Works   Using Power Lister   Privacy
Tech Support   Add a Link

Each auction supported by Power Lister is copyrighted and is a Registered Trademark (TM) of its parent corporation.

Best experienced with GoToWorld, Netscape 4.0, or Internet Explorer 4.0 or better.
Copyright © 1999 Power Lister. Power Lister powered by LinkJump and J2KGifts.
LinkJump is owned and operated by Unique Stuff, Inc.

CHAPTER 11
Digital Strategies

A very important aspect of online auction success, and one that is overlooked by too many sellers, is preparing your photographs properly. I'm not just talking about the quality of the picture itself, but of the characteristics of the digital file that is your photo. I've seen (as I'm sure you have) many photos that are way too big to fit my browser window, way too big in size so as to take precious minutes to load, photos that were sideways and upside down, and images with "screen door" patterns in them. Most scanners and digital cameras come with software for image editing, and all of these problems can be done away with in a very short period of time.

If you do not have any image editing software, it's not difficult to come by. The most powerful program for manipulating graphic images is Adobe Photoshop. Photoshop is used by the vast majority of graphic art professionals working in the printing and Web design industries, but with the power comes a price—full versions cost about $550. If you are in the market for a scanner you can sometimes find deals where Photoshop comes bundled with the scanner, and the net effect is that of getting the scanner for free. Just be sure that if you purchase a scanner that comes bundled with Photoshop, and you are paying in the neighborhood of $550, you are getting the full version. Some scanners ship with Photoshop LE (limited edition), a scaled-down version.

Adobe also makes a less expensive image-editing package, Adobe PhotoDeluxe. Tryout versions of many Adobe programs, including Photoshop, can be downloaded for free at *http://www.adobe.com*. Tryout versions do not allow you to save, export or print artwork.

Another option is to go with shareware, and a popular shareware image editor can be downloaded for a free trial at *http://www.jasc.com*. The program is Paint Shop Pro, and if you like what you see during the evaluation period you can purchase the most recent full version (version 5.03 as of 8/25/99) for $99. An earlier version (version 3.12) with fewer features is also available for $69. Version 6 of Paint Shop Pro is already available to download as a beta. Beta programs are still in the testing stages, and while most are quite stable if you don't like surprises or wrestling with program bugs stick to the earlier versions.

Let's examine the major issues with successful online photographs, and the methods of treating each problem for maximum results. When striving to get the best photo in the least amount of file space, you should attack the first three items in the exact order they are presented here—Resolution-Cropping-Photo Dimensions.

Resolution

Resolution, as it applies to digital images, is the ability of the software to capture and display clarity of features and light diffusion. The higher the resolution of an image, the more detail and contrast you should be able to see. Resolution is important in the traditional printing process, where it is measured in dots per inch (dpi). If you have ever looked at a printed photograph under a magnifying glass, you know it is made up of a series of dots. Logically the more dots you cram into one square inch of space, the more detail those extra dots can exhibit. However, the more dots you have, the larger your file becomes, and on the Internet file space is important because it relates to how long a picture takes to load into a potential bidder's browser.

While the technology exists to scan photographs using resolutions of over 1000 dpi, in practical use there is no good reason to do so because the human eye begins to lose its ability to discern the increased detail at 300 dpi. That being the case, nearly every photograph you see in every quality book and magazine has been scanned at 300 dpi—there just isn't a need to go higher because most people won't notice much difference.

The same principles apply to photographs that are being used on the Internet. Nearly every computer monitor ever produced displays images at approximately 72 dpi—that is the resolution of the screen display. Therefore, scanning images at more than 72 dpi resolution for viewing on the Internet has limited, if any, value. The extra detail gained by scanning at higher resolutions is lost in the translation from file to screen. If I haven't confused you too much, you've figured out by now that there is no good reason to scan your photos at a resolution higher than 72 dpi. Your scanner software will let you control the resolution setting—adjust it to 72 dpi.

What about setting resolutions for digital cameras? While most don't have the capability of designating a numerical resolution, they do offer several quality settings. If you select the low quality setting for your digital images, you are probably getting 72 dpi, or something very similar.

Your image editing software will give you the ability to change the resolutions of your images. Look under the Edit menu of your software for Image Size, Image Resolution, or something similar. You should be able to control the resolution for existing files in this way. By using a resolution of 72 dpi instead of 300 dpi, for example, you can potentially decrease the amount of time it takes your photo to load over a 56K modem by as much as a minute.

Cropping

Cropping is trimming away parts of the photograph that are not necessary to show your item completely. Usually when you scan a photo or take a picture with a digital camera, there is more image than is actually necessary to get your message across. Cropping allows you to control what part of the photograph you actually use, and is another way to reduce the file size of your photo.

Often the cropping tool is found on a toolbar that displays when your image editing software is launched—if you can't find it consult your program documentation or go to the Help menu and look for "Crop". Once activated, your mouse is used to outline the area you want to keep. Position your mouse in the upper right corner of your photo, click, and drag. A box will form that changes size depending on how far you move your mouse. Once you release the mouse the box will become permanent; however you can alter all four sides of it by positioning the mouse over a side, and clicking and dragging again. Once the box outlines just the part of the photo you want, go under the Image menu and select Crop, or follow the instructions that came with your particular software package. Everything outside the box will be deleted, leaving just the necessary part of your photo and effectively reducing it in size.

Photo Dimensions

In the digital world, the size of your photo corresponds to changes in the resolution. You will notice that when you use your image editing software to change the resolution of an existing image from 300 dpi to 72 dpi, the *pixel dimensions* of the image will also change.

Pixels are simply very small units of displayable information—similar in a way to the dots in a traditional printed photograph. When viewing images on a computer monitor we are concerned with pixel dimensions—if we alter pixels we also alter the photograph characteristics as they apply to color, content, or size. Altering pixels is the principle on which image software works, giving us the ability to change reds to blues, bushes to trees, and images that are too large to images that are just right.

While 17-inch monitors are becoming more common as the computer revolution continues, many of us are still using the 15-inch variety with the screen area set to 640x480. This means that if the pixel dimensions of your photograph exceed 640 wide and 480 high, many of us won't be able to view your entire photograph on our screen without scrolling. A photo that can't be viewed in its entirety gives a skewed perspective of your item, and is in many ways more detrimental than having the photo too small.

To correct this problem, begin by checking the resolution of the photo. If it is more than 72 dpi, as outlined above, change the resolution to 72 dpi. This may be enough to resize your photo to acceptable dimensions. If it's already at 72 dpi, or if it is still larger than 640x480 after you adjust the resolution, you will have to physically change the pixel dimensions of the photo with your image editing software. You should be able to accomplish this by clicking on Image Size, found under the Edit menu of many image editing programs. Simply replace the existing Width and Height dimensions with smaller ones. If you need guidelines, try for photographs that are no more than 300x300 height and width, and 60K in size.

Photo Patterns

Have you ever looked at a photo of a postcard on the Internet only to see a pattern that made you think you were looking at it through a screen door? In the printing industry this is called a moiré pattern—it occurs when an original that has already been printed once, and is therefore formed by a series of angled dots, is scanned again, introducing new dots on potentially different angles. There are several methods you can use to tackle this problem, one in particular comes with a tradeoff you will have to assess.

If you are using a digital camera you more than likely won't encounter this. The technology is not the same as doing an actual scan, and the camera should not produce objectionable patterns. Taking photos of printed materials has its own problems, however. Often the perspective will be off due to the curve of the lens or the angle of the camera to the original, causing a squared off item like a postcard to look bowed, or sometimes more narrow at one end than the other. These fluctuations in perspective can be noted in your item description, assuring potential bidders that the card indeed has square corners.

If you're scanning, there is a good chance your scanner software has a filter you can use to alleviate, if not eliminate, the pattern. For instance Microtek, with its ScanWizard software, allows you to choose from several *descreening* options: Newspaper, Magazine, Art Magazine, and Custom. Selecting the Magazine option will work for most printed material, and eliminates the objectionable pattern altogether.

If you don't have filters with your scanner software, or if you can't find a setting that gets rid of the screen pattern, there's one more "trick" you can try. Open the photo with your image editing software and look for an option called Blur. If you know how to sharpen your photos, blur will probably be on the same menu—it is in essence the opposite of sharpen. Often if you apply the Blur filter to your photo, the objectionable pattern will be softened. The tradeoff, of course, is that the rest of your photo will be softened also. You will have to decide which is the lesser of two evils, a pattern or a slightly out of focus photo.

Color Correction/Contrast

Many dealers tell me they never have to worry about the quality of their images because their digital cameras do such a good job of capturing the original. While this is true to an extent, as long as you have your photo editing software launched and are cropping and sizing, it doesn't hurt to take a minute and try one more thing.

Most image editing software has a feature called Auto Levels, or something similar, found under the Image menu. By selecting it, the software interprets the saturation and contrast levels in the photograph and makes automatic adjustments. You might be surprised at how much better your photo looks once this feature is applied. If you don't like the result, you should be able to Undo it under the Edit menu. I'm betting you will like what you see more often than you don't.

There are a wide variety of tools available to change the color and contrast of your photos manually. While they can be fun to learn and beneficial in a few cases, for the most part you should leave this type of image manipulation to the graphic artists of the world. Once you know what the software is capable of, it's hard not to spend too much time making your photos look better. Remember: you don't need a masterpiece for your online auction listing—besides, color is entirely subjective. What may look fabulous to you could look entirely different to someone else, making your foray into the world of digital rendering a waste of time—time you could have spent at an auction finding more stuff to sell!

CHAPTER 12
Keeping Records for People Who Hate to Keep Records

This will be a short chapter, because this is really easy. While I am not a bulk seller on the Internet auctions, I do on many occasions have 15-20 items listed at the same time. The system I am about to show you has served me well and you can refine it even more to suit your needs.

Let me start by saying that I have been around computers for a long time—since the early 1970s when I worked with the first word processors to hit the market (anybody remember Wang?). I know computers and technology, and frankly sometimes they aren't necessary! If you are a bulk seller you will probably want to keep records using a spreadsheet program that automatically calculates sums for you, along with accounting software. As a bulk seller, you likely have an employee or two that can input the data for you, or who can take care of other things while you do it. For most of us the system I am about to share is adequate. If you are a dealer that needs numbers at tax time, at the end of each week, month, quarter, or even year, you can sit down with your calculator and arrive at your profit/loss numbers for your online auction business relatively quickly.

The materials you will need to undertake this system of record keeping are a three-ring binder with a 3-inch spine and five divider pages and, well, that's about it, other than some standard office supplies like a 3-hole punch, a stapler, a pencil, and some tape.

First, label the five divider pages and place them in the notebook in this order...1) Purchases-Need Check. 2) Purchases-Check Sent. 3) Purchases-Completed. 4) Sales-Pending. 5) Sales-Completed. Now it's just a matter of printing out the first page of every auction you win and every auction you list (if you want a photo record of the item you may have to print more than one page, but I haven't found a photo record necessary). Wait until the auctions end to print them out so you have a record of the seller or high bidder. Punch the printouts to go in the binder, and write on the printout any additional information you want to keep. When auction acknowledgement e-mails are received, print them also and add them to the notebook, stapled to the appropriate auction listing.

Here's one example. If you are the high bidder on an item, print out the auction page and, somewhere on the printout, make a notation of when the seller contacted you with his address information. Keep it simple—come up with an abbreviated coding system, for instance SC7/20/99 means seller contact July 20th, 1999 by my system. If you pay by check, I like using the checks that make automatic carbon copies when you write them. That way, you can just staple the copy of the check right to the paperwork. If you don't use carbon copy checks, go with another code—CK132-7/21/99$25.00 could signify check #132 dated July 21, 1999 in the amount of $25.00. Once the check is written and the payment mailed, move your listing to the "Purchases-Check Sent" part of your notebook.

When the item is received, I don't even bother to record the date—I haven't found a good enough reason to warrant doing it because I always (OK, usually) remember that it has arrived. If you're a volume seller and/or have employees working for you, I'd recommend you make it a policy to record the received date on the auction printout. If an employee gets the package you might not even realize it has arrived without a record.

Sometimes I don't get a chance to leave feedback right away. By simply browsing through the "Purchases-Check Sent" category in the notebook I can pull out the items that have arrived, leave feedback for them all at one sitting, and then file them in the "Purchases-Completed" section of the notebook. If you keep a separate record of how much you pay for resale items, update it now. Don't forget to add your shipping costs to the purchase price—shipping should be considered as part of the cost of merchandise.

Now let's look at another example when you are selling instead of buying. After the auction closes, print out the auction so you have a record of the high bidder and place it in the "Sales-Pending" part of the notebook. If they are using an eBay™ ID that is not their e-mail address, first click on their ID as if you were going to e-mail them. A screen will appear asking you for your registered eBay™ name and password—fill them in and click the "Remember Me" box before submitting the request. Once the request is accepted, you can e-mail the high bidder with your address information and shipping costs if you are ready to do that. But the real point of this exercise was to expose e-mail addresses—now if you use the Back button of your browser to go back to the listing, the e-mail address will appear behind the User ID (if it doesn't, just hit Refresh and it will). From this point on, until you close your browser window, e-mail addresses will appear behind User ID's.

Somewhere on the printout where you have enough room (the lower right corner if possible—you'll see why later) record your cost of acquisition (COA), sales price (SP), and net profit (NP). At the end of the month or quarter you can quickly thumb through these printouts, adding the columns of numbers to give you an idea of how you're doing and at the same time preparing for the tax man.

So you have a printout of the closed auction that shows the final bid price and the e-mail address of the high bidder, as well as your required tax information. I don't record the date I contact the high bidder, but that's up to you. Since I usually send shipping information within 24 hours, knowing that is enough when I already have the auction close date on the printout.

Next, write the shipping/handling cost you quoted the high bidder. On large, heavy items I often give the high bidder the option of either priority mail or parcel post—having a record of the amount you quoted tells you which method to use when shipping the package based on the amount of their check. It also alerts you if the buyer underpays. Use the coding system again—in my system S/H/I$34.50 means the cost of shipping, handling, and insurance is $34.50. PP/H/I$34.50 means the same thing, but the shipping method is parcel post.

When the check arrives, record the date you received it, the check number, the amount of the check, and whether or not payment for insurance was included, again right on the printout. I would also recommend packing the item at this time—unless the check bounces you now know the transaction will be fulfilled. If the item has been insured, write the amount of insurance to take out beside your name in the return address area of the package. That way, when you do take the package to the post office to ship it, you will know how much to insurance it for. If insure has not been purchased, write "NO" instead of an amount. Then move the paperwork to the front of the "Sales-Pending" section if no other items are waiting to ship, or just behind the paperwork of items you have already received checks for so that the checks received earliest are still on top. Now by simply browsing the "Sales-Pending" section you can keep track of when items are due to ship—most sellers wait 7-10 business days to allow time for the check to clear.

When shipping day comes, if the item is insured make sure you get an insurance receipt from the post office. Simply tape it or staple it to the auction listing printout. Once that is done, move the printout to the "Sales-Completed" part of the notebook. Remove all of the paperwork monthly, quarterly, or at any time increment that fits your book keeping methods and file it away with your other important documents.

As easy as this system is, some of you will still want to experiment with using accounting software. Two programs you will want to investigate are QuickBooks 99 (*http://www.quickbooks.com*) and Peachtree Office Accounting (*http://www.peachtree.com*). While QuickBooks 99 is considered the easiest to use, Peachtree Office Accounting offers a more powerful interface at a lower price. QuickBooks 99 also offers a free downloadable version, good for 25 sessions. The data you record during those sessions can be saved, and upon purchasing QuickBooks 99 you simply "unlock" the trial version and can retain your data.

CHAPTER 13
To Employ, or not to Employ

Taking on an employee is a big decision. There are pros and cons to be weighed, and just as important is to know your personality. If you're the type who feels that a job isn't done right unless you do it yourself, you probably won't be satisfied with any employee you hire. The antiques and collectibles business is full of dealers who work alone, but the Internet has opened up the possibility of new income streams, and some of us will need employees to take full advantage.

According to government statistics, unemployment figures are lower in 1999 than they have been for 25 years. Consequently, skilled workers are not readily available. But you already know that selling on the Internet is not rocket science, and if you are willing to train a novice you should be able to find an employee that will work out fine.

Why would you want to hire an employee? The biggest reason is the time it takes to list and sell items on the Internet, which takes time away from the responsibilities of running your business. If you expect to list more than 20-25 items daily you should definitely consider hiring, even if it's on a part time basis. Otherwise you will spend all of your time behind the computer instead of finding new inventory, keeping the books, or managing your traditional outlets.

Let's break down the Internet auction selling process into components and then examine the processes that you should handle yourself and those you can hire out:

1. Acquisition of inventory
2. Repairs and cleaning of items
3. Pricing
4. Photographing or scanning
5. Image editing
6. Image uploading
7. Writing descriptions
8. Listing
9. Answering e-mail questions for potential buyers
10. Packing/shipping
11. Calculating shipping costs
12. Notifying winning bidders
13. Leaving feedback

Acquisition of Inventory—Of course this is one you'll want to keep doing yourself. Unless you're lucky enough to hire an employee who is familiar with the type of merchandise you sell, the buying is up to you. If you use online auctions to purchase for resale, your employee can act as your sniper when you can't be at the computer yourself. Give them a limit on an item and have them watch it while doing other things and place that last minute bid that often can win the merchandise.

Repairs and cleaning—Here's one that can be turned over to your employee, particularly if they're handy. Getting items cleaned up for resale is no big deal, but making repairs might be depending on the degree of difficulty in the repairs you usually tackle yourself. If you're a dealer looking to do volume, you shouldn't buy items that consume lots of time to repair, like major refinishing jobs or broken clocks. But if you do less extensive work, like furniture touch-up as opposed to refinishing, your employee can be trained to do most of it.

Pricing—You should keep control of this area, setting the prices using your experience in the marketplace and whatever formula you use for your profit margin. Don't expect an employee to know how to price merchandise—chances are you will be disappointed at the results.

Photographing or scanning—Delegate this to an employee. You might have to do a bit of training, particularly if you use a flatbed scanner instead of a digital camera, but the time you save by not having this responsibility will be well worth it. The photos you use to sell online don't have to be museum quality—in fact they shouldn't be (see Chapter 11—Digital Strategies)—and most people can adapt easily to taking pictures with either a digital camera or scanning conventional photos.

Image editing—Another task for you to delegate. Some online sellers skip this step altogether, but I don't recommend it. If you've ever impatiently waited for an oversized image to load and finally decided you didn't need to bid on it that badly, you'll know what I mean. Your photos should be edited for size, cropping, and resolution at the very least (see Chapter 11—Digital Strategies).

Image uploading—Don't waste your precious time with this function. Uploading photos is easy, regardless of how intimidating it seems to beginners. Once you train someone to use an FTP program it soon becomes a no-brainer. And if you use the free photo hosting services the chore becomes even easier.

Writing descriptions—We're back in your court again. The title you use for your auction, as well as the description, are the two most important factors in drawing bidders to you and realizing high prices. You alone should take the responsibility to make sure they are correct and well prepared. Be sure your title contains key words that a collector of your item might enter as a search parameter in the auction search engine. If the item has a brand name, use it in the title. The description should contain detailed facts about size, color, composition and condition as well as your terms of sale (who pays shipping, if insurance is required, etc.). I also strongly recommend you include your sales policy, particularly as it pertains to returns. If you don't want it as part of your description, create a separate HTML page and provide a link to it from your auction descriptions.

Listing—You've written the title and description and priced the item. Your employee can take that information and do the actual listing. Make up a blank form that includes categories your employee needs from you to activate a listing. Copy the form, retaining at least one blank to make future copies from. Then just fill in the information your employee needs and hand them over. You can even design a form that continues to serve as your paperwork for that item—have the employee fill in the auction item ID number once it is listed and any other information you like to have. At the end of the auction the employee can fill in the final bid price and high bidder ID. If you like having a paper trail in case the IRS comes knocking, this type of system makes sense. Check your word processing program—you'll probably find that you can create a blank template to use over and over, and you can then fill in the blanks on your computer instead of writing them out for each listing.

Answering e-mail questions for potential bidders—I have been told by some dealers that this is the most time consuming part of the job for them. Personally, I believe that if you are getting that many questions you aren't doing a good enough job with your descriptions. I haven't had a question about one of my listings for months, because I follow my own rules about the importance of the description. Nonetheless, this is a job your employee can handle as long as you make them understand that if they have even 1% of doubt about the answer they are giving, they should talk to you before clicking the "Send" button.

Packing/shipping—This should be an employee duty, and the packing can be done as soon as you know the item is sold (after the first bid, or once it meets reserve). Occasionally the same bidder purchases more than one item, causing you to unpack and repack in one box to save shipping costs, but this doesn't happen often so go ahead and get packages ready early on if you can. The item should definitely be properly packed before weighing to get shipping costs. When it's time to ship, have the employee take the packages to the post office and pay by check, returning with a cash receipt.

Calculating shipping costs—Employee duty. You need to supply an accurate scale, and make sure the employee knows that the item must be packed before weighing. You might be surprised how much difference a box and some packing material can make in weight. Ask at your local post office for a chart that gives shipping costs by weight. Or, your employee can visit *http://www.usps.gov* to calculate accurate shipping costs (I recommend the U.S. post office for all shipping). If you're shipping a heavy package, or if the buyer asks you to check the cost of parcel post shipping, it can be done from this site also. You must have their zip code to be accurate in these cases.

Notifying winning bidders—Your employee can do this one too. My recommendation would be for you to compose a high bidder notification as a word processing document. Make it generic enough that your employee can call it up, copy it, and then paste it into e-mail messages, having to change only a few words in each message to identify the item and perhaps item number. Here's what I use—the words that ***definitely*** need to change each time are highlighted in bold italic. Words that *might* need to change each time are in regular italic, and of course use your own name and address.

Greetings from Western Maryland!

Congratulations on being high bidder for the ***1939 Worlds Fair paperweight*** (eBay #***123456789***). Please add *$3.20* to your high bid for priority mail shipping. Insurance (if you want it-your choice) would be an additional *$0.85*. Send check or money order to...

John Doe
1000 Main Street
Anywhere, USA

Please respond to this message with your full name and address so I know you have received the information and I can get your package ready.

Merchandise paid by money order is shipped within 24-48 hours of receipt. Merchandise paid by check is held until the check clears, usually 7-10 business days. Out-of-U.S. buyers please contact me for revised shipping rates.

Thanks
John

This message can be applied to multiple bidder notifications with very little editing. Once the message is copied to your computer's clipboard, you can paste it over and over, making just the changes required for each different bidder.

Leaving feedback—Again, your employee can handle this. The vast majority of feedback messages you leave will be positive and similar, so you can prepare a few "stock" messages and instruct the employee to use the most appropriate one.

As you can see, of the thirteen major functions we identified to fulfill an online auction listing, you need only keep control of three of them. That leaves ten for your employee to handle efficiently. After all, if you're going to pay someone, they should earn it!

If you do decide to hire, check with temp services in your area and discuss the benefits of obtaining employees through them. Most will handle the necessary paperwork that goes with hiring employees so you don't have to trade off the time you save with the time you spend doing paperwork for the government.

Another option to soften the burden of being an employer is to hire independent contractors—they are responsible for keeping their own records. If you plan to hire just periodic or seasonal help, this should work fine. I don't recommend trying to hire a part time employee in this way though—it's one of those things that puts up a red-flag to the IRS. And keep in mind that if you pay an independent contractor over $600.00 in a single calendar year, you must file a 1099 form on their behalf.

I could probably write another book about the laws governing the hiring and firing of employees and how to protect yourself. In most cases, if you communicate clearly and make sure your employee knows what is expected of them you'll be fine. Don't forget to praise when praise is due, and apply the golden rule and treat your employee(s) as you would like to be treated—in most cases you will be rewarded. If you're not, keep good records of what you believe to be inappropriate behavior and use this three-step process with your employee if the behavior continues:

1. Give them a verbal warning
2. Give them a written warning
3. Termination

Don't be afraid to terminate an employment situation and find someone who does the job to your satisfaction. Working through a temp service can also make this unpleasant task more manageable.

Chapter 14
Rules and Regulations

The Internet Tax Freedom Act was introduced in March 1997 and has undergone several changes since. The basis of the act is that electronic commerce should be a tariff-free zone, free from tariffs and discriminatory taxes. As of now, a moratorium in force until October 21, 2001 prohibits states from taxing Internet access and imposing other discriminatory taxes on e-commerce. You can read the full text of this important doctrine at *http://www.house.gov/chriscox/nettax/lawsums.html*.

Do not confuse the Internet Tax Freedom act with freedom from paying taxes on merchandise you sell online. While it is true that the Internet is, as of late 1999, largely unregulated, there are some rules you must follow to keep your business legal. Some are general rules associated with any business, others are site-specific rules for what you can and cannot sell. Unregulated or not make no mistake—the IRS *is* watching.

Making a Federal Case

Nothing is for sure except death and taxes, and I suspect mankind has a better chance of beating death than we do the tax system. You must keep records of your online sales profits to be claimed at tax time. The good news is that, along with sales income, there are business deductions you don't want to overlook that can help reduce your tax burden.

The IRS has a useful and informative Web site at *http://www irs.ustreas.gov* where you can find the answers to many of your business-related questions. While operating your new business does add some stress to filing your tax return, if you keep good records (see Chapter 12—Keeping Records for People Who Hate to Keep Records) you can still do it yourself.

As a sole proprietor you will need to file a Schedule C in addition to your 1040 form. If your business has net income you will also be required to file a Schedule SE. If you engage in a partnership or form a corporation, I would suggest at least considering the services of a professional to do your taxes. You not only get the benefit of having someone in your court who can find all deductions you are entitled to, you avoid the problems that invariably come into play when more than one person is involved in making decisions for the business.

If your income is strictly from self-employment, you also will have to estimate the tax you will owe on a quarterly basis and submit payments to both the IRS and your state taxing authority. Both of these entities will have information available on how to do this, and the Federal tax form you will use is a 1040ES. State forms vary by state, so be sure you inquire.

Deductions? What Deductions?

Make sure you are taking full advantage of the deductions available to you by (ugh) reading the appropriate IRS forms and perhaps even purchasing a tax book or two. If you have a friend in the tax preparation business, ask for free advice. We will talk about the major deductions here, but tax laws change and this cannot be considered a complete list.

Home Office Deduction—If you conduct your business from your home, you are probably entitled to take a deduction for the expenses incurred for operating the portion of your home that houses your office. The amount you can deduct is determined by the percentage of space your home office occupies. For instance, if you live in a 10,000 square foot home and the area used *exclusively* for your office takes up 2,000 square feet, you will be entitled to claim 20% of the costs of running your home, including utilities, taxes, etc. Keep in mind that in some cases you can write off the entire expense, such as when you have a separate phone, fax, or modem line into your office that is used only for your business.

Office Equipment Deduction—Any equipment you purchase for use with your business can be expensed, or depreciated over time. This applies to computers, printers, fax machines, copiers, modems—almost any piece of equipment that contributes to the operation of your business. This deduction softens the blow of major purchases a bit—while it does you no good when you're laying out the cash initially, it is at least a comfort to know that a few of those dollars will be returning to you at tax time.

Here's how it works. If you purchase a new multipurpose printer/fax/scanner and expect it to have a useful life of four years, you can deduct 25% of the cost of the equipment each year each of those next four years. You do not get the entire 25% back each year, but rather the deduction is applied against your other income to reduce your tax burden. If the equipment purchase cost $5,000, your deduction would be $1250 each year for each of the next four years. If your income in those years was $50,000, you would pay tax on $48,750 instead of the full $50,000. While this might not sound like a big deal, throw in a few more deductions (particularly the home office deduction mentioned earlier) and your taxable income will be significantly reduced.

I must mention here that to be "perfectly legal" you must use any equipment you fully depreciate *exclusively* for business purposes. If your spouse also uses the equipment to print out personal e-mail messages, or to fax relatives maps showing them how to find your house on their summer vacation, you must arrive at a percentage of business use versus personal use and depreciate only the percentage used for business. At this point you can usually get by with taking your best educated guess as to percentages. I expect in the future there will be software that keeps track of business versus personal time in these areas.

Also be aware that some states have a *personal property tax* that is assessed against these same assets that you are deducting. If you're going to claim them as deductions, you may also have to pay tax on them. As ludicrous as this sounds it is fact but thankfully the depreciation savings usually outweigh the tax. Ever heard the expression "they get you coming and going?"

Mileage Deduction—The miles you put on your car or truck for business purposes can be deducted. That includes every trip you make to go to an auction, flea market, or yard sale to acquire merchandise for resale. It also includes trips to the store for business supplies, or deliveries if you offer to deliver large items within a certain distance of your home. To use this deduction keep good records—this is one that the IRS watches closely. Keep a log book in your vehicle and record the mileage on your vehicle at the beginning of the year, the amount of mileage recorded for each business trip, and the mileage at the end of the year. At tax time use the beginning and ending numbers to determine total mileage, and your other log entries to determine how much of that mileage was business related. Even if your vehicle is used for both business and personal use, you may deduct the amount of mileage used for business as long as you keep good records.

Office Supplies Deduction—Once you invest in new office equipment your focus will switch to maintaining it so it runs properly. The purchase price of printer ink cartridges, copier paper, ZIP disks, service contracts, and even everyday items like tape and paper clips, can be deducted at tax time. You may well be able to deduct the cost of this book, as well as other price guides and books that assist you in producing income.

Internet Fees Deduction—Much of the cost of doing business on the Internet is probably deductible. This includes the monthly charge you pay for access as well as the fees you pay to list items with online auctions.

Accountant Fees Deduction—If you do choose to retain the services of an accountant to do your book keeping, you can deduct their fee. Keep in mind that if you retain an accountant to do your taxes for 1999, his work will actually take place in the year 2000 and you will not be able to take the deduction until you file your year 2000 tax return.

Licensed Guides

There is currently a debate going on in a neighboring community to the small town where I live as to whether or not any new home businesses will be allowed to operate there. The local lawmakers voted some time back to disallow any new applications, and once the news hit the street there was pandemonium.

To avoid being trapped in a legal tangle you don't want or need, check with your local city or county clerk's office to find out what steps you need to take in order to be recognized as a legal home business in your area. There are zoning laws to be considered as well as licenses that you might need. We both know that there are thousands of people earning extra money from the safety of their living rooms on the Internet. Don't be the one that gets caught doing something illegal.

State Sales Tax

I'm going to leave it up to you to know and understand the law that governs sales tax in your state. Whatever applies to your sales at the local mall where you have a booth, or the local shows you do, also applies to your Internet sales. I can give you some help in the form of an Internet address for a page with links to state tax Web sites for every state. You can visit your state tax site and get information and forms online. Just point your browser to *http://www.bakershore.com/bsatable.htm* for the links.

In most cases, obeying the sales tax law equates to charging the appropriate state sales tax to buyers who reside in the same state in which you operate your business, unless they furnish you a copy of their tax exempt certificate. The fact that you do charge sales tax should be included as part of your auction description, and can be automatically inserted by both AuctionAssistant2 and AuctionPoster98, two auction posting software packages reviewed in Chapter 8—Auction Enhancing Software.

In most cases, if you ship the merchandise to another state, sales tax need not be collected. Be aware of the individual tax laws in your state of residence—some have unusual rules. In Maryland for instance, a dealer must spend $200 in a single transaction before they legally become tax exempt. Collect sales tax and record it as you would any other sale, submitting it with your quarterly sales use tax form. If you don't currently have a sales tax number for yourself or your business, visit your local tax office to find out how to apply for one. You may also be able to get information on how to apply from a dealer at your local antique mall.

In addition to tax regulations, most online auction sites prohibit the sale of certain items. Following are restrictions for some of the major online auctions.

eBay™ Restrictions

eBay™ has the following rules prohibiting the sale of certain items on their site. The information was gleaned from numerous files on the eBay™ Web site. This should not be considered a complete list—visit *http://pages-new.ebay.com/help/sellerguide /index.html* and run a search for *prohibited items* for more information and updates.

Firearms, weapons, and accessories
Any and all firearms, including air guns
Any and all military weapons (including but not limited to bazookas, grenades, mortars)
Any and all explosives
Ammunition with propellant, including any armor-piercing bullets
Firearm kits (any kit able to create a firearm)
Gunpowder
Illegal weapons (including but not limited to switchblades over 2 inches, brass knuckles)
Silencers
Software
Beta or pre-release software
Original Equipment Manufacturer software sold separately from its bundled hardware

Pirated software, including unlicensed backup copies and modchips
Software licensed for educational use only

Entertainment
Movies or music in pre-release stage
Promotional CDs, tapes, or albums
Unauthorized copies of movies or music, including concert recordings

Miscellaneous
Bulk e-mail addresses
Counterfeit items
Descramblers, including cable television and satellite dish
Embargoed items
False ID
Human remains
Illegal animal parts
Illegal drugs, including drug paraphernalia
Listings requiring winning bidders to purchase additional items or services
Listings charging excessive shipping or handling fees
Listings selling only minimally valued items to advertise non-eBay sales
Listings claiming the listed item is illegal
Live animals
Police badges, including unauthorized copies of police badges or ID
Skulls
Soiled underwear (believe it or not this came about because some ladies were buying pantyhose, wearing them, and offering them for sale. Obviously there were buyers or this rule would not have been necessary)

Amazon.com Auctions Restrictions

Amazon.com Auctions has the following rules prohibiting the sale of certain items on their site. This should not be considered a complete list—log in, go to Seller Services, and click on *Prohibited Content* for more information and updates.

Any and all pornography
Firearms and ammunition
Homemade alcoholic beverages
Items deemed illegal by any applicable law

Items that are clearly intended wholly or mainly as portals to commercial or private Web sites for the purposes of advertising
Items that infringe on another party's copyright, patent, trademark or other proprietary right, including rights of publicity and privacy
Listings using miscategorization and/or inappropriate cross-selling
Living creatures
Offensive material, including hate literature
Stolen goods

Auction Universe Restrictions

Auction Universe has the following rules prohibiting the sale of certain items on their site. This should not be considered a complete list—log in, and review the Rules of the Road—The Auction document for more information and updates.

Listings containing adult matter, including explicit language and photographs
Merchandise or services that infringe anyone's copyright, trademark, patent or other proprietary rights
Counterfeit or other illegal items
Merchandise or services that are illegal for you to sell in the circumstances of your auction under any local, state, federal or international law, statute, ordinance or regulation
Auctions containing pornographic or similarly objectionable content, links, pictures, banners, or language
Merchandise or services that infringe or violate anyone's rights of privacy or publicity
Instructions to perform an illegal activity or procure merchandise or services in an illegal manner
Stolen merchandise
Domestic animals
Merchandise or services, which if sold through us, would cause us to violate any applicable local, state, federal or international law, statute, ordinance or regulation

Yahoo! Auctions Restrictions

Yahoo! Auctions has the following rules prohibiting the sale of certain items on their site. This should not be considered a complete list—log in, go to Sellers Guide and click on "What am I not allowed to sell?" for more information and updates.

Any item that is illegal to sell under any applicable law, statute, ordinance, or regulation
Items that you do not have the legal right to sell
Any item that infringes or violates anyone's rights
Live animals
Food (other than packaged food meeting all applicable federal, state, and local standards for sale to consumers by commercial merchants)
Alcoholic beverages (except if you are reselling an alcoholic beverage that was initially purchased from a retailer and is still in its original container and it is legal to deliver into the jurisdiction where the buyer lives)
Cigarettes
Stolen goods
Firearms
Any item which, in Yahoo!'s sole discretion, is inflammatory, offensive, or otherwise inconsistent with the spirit of Yahoo! Auctions

GoMainLine.com Restrictions

GoMainLine.com is more general with their restrictions, reserving the right to prohibit any item(s) they consider illegal or offensive. The GoMainLine.com restrictions can be found on the rules and customs page *http://www.gomainline. com/ml/ezstart/ez_rules.asp* and reads as follows...

Mainline reserves the right to remove any item listed for auction/sale for any reason at our sole discretion. Do not list items for auction/sale that you do not have the right to sell. Don't list stolen items. Ask Mainline first if you are unsure. We will fully cooperate with law enforcement authorities to prevent and investigate any violations.

Appendix A

Internet Antiques and Collectibles Sites

This is not a complete listing of antiques and collectibles sites available on the Internet. There are new sites arriving regularly, as well as some closing shop—it is literally impossible to publish a complete list and have it stay current for more than a few days. The sites listed in this Appendix will give you a broad sampling of the best places to buy and sell online—there is more than enough variety here to give you the tools you need to be successful.

Multi-Dealer Malls and Shops

American Antique Mall
http://www.elegantantiques.com
American Antiques Mall offers a selection of antiques and collectibles in online antique dealer booths. Primarily, the offerings are depression glass and pottery.

Antique Alley
http://www.bmark.com/aa/
Over 100 independent dealers, each with an online catalog, a search engine to help you locate what you're looking for, and a comprehensive directory of traditional antique shops with their snail-mail addresses.

collect.com
http://www.csmonline.com/buysell/
Thousands of items offered by hundreds of merchants. Browse categories or search by keyword(s).

Collector Online
http://www.collectoronline.com
A major Internet mall, with over 200 dealers. An innovative online Inventory Management System (IMS) allows you to catalog an unlimited number of items and send them to eBay™, Auction Universe, Yahoo! Auctions, or your Collector Online booth with the click of a mouse.

GoUniq.com
http://www.gouniq.com
Multiple dealers with fixed prices.

Ruby Lane
http://www.rubylane.com
An excellent antiques and collectibles search engine, as well as a place to build your online storefront and display your merchandise for sale.

The Internet Antique Store
http://www.tias.com
One of the largest antiques and collectibles malls on the Internet. Links to over 190 dealers and a search engine make shopping fun and easy.

Online Auctions

aBros™
http://www.abros.net
A general auction site with antiques, collectibles, coins, glass, and a lot of Beanie Babies. An auction staff member will post your photos for you for $3.00 each if you e-mail the photos to them.

Amazon.com Auctions
http://auctions.amazon.com
The "World's Biggest Bookstore" has entered the online auction world. Amazon.com offers a buyer's guarantee that says you will receive your item and it will be as described by the seller, or they will refund your purchase price up to a $250.00 limit.

America's Auctions and Sales
http://www.aaands.com
Antiques, collectibles, dolls, hobbies, and toys are a few of the categories you will find here. Visit the Gold Room, where items with opening bids exceeding $1,000.00 are listed in one place and bid on an 18th century tapestry or a 1990 Chevy Geo.

AuctionAddict
http://www.auctionaddict.com
Auction addict bills themselves as "a person-to-person auction and classified ads venue with no listing fees." You can also create your own storefront from their site.

AuctionPort
http://www.auctionport.com
Auction Port says they never impose a basic insertion or listing fee and the service is always free to the buyer, and they claim over one million page hits by unique users each week. They also offer an associates program for increased exposure, and you can have your own private auction room.

Auction Universe
http://www.auctionuniverse.com
An optional program called BidSafe™ helps assure satisfactory transactions with a minimum of fraud. Credit card information is utilized by Auction Universe to automatically charge buyer purchases, assuring the seller of funds. The charge is refunded by Auction Universe if the merchandise never arrives.

Auctionworks
http://www.auctionworks.com
Auctionworks bills themselves as "Antiques, Computers, Collectibles, and more..." A well designed and easy to navigate site that, like many others, is struggling to gain a foothold on eBay™'s beach by offering free listings if your item does not sell.

A1Auction
http://www.a1auction.com
Officially launched September 20, 1998, A1 Auction specializes in flea market items. You can find anything from Egyptian papyrus to computer processors—and if you're in the market for a 37mm grenade launcher you might find it here!

BoxLot
http://www.boxlot.com
Not really box lots in the auction sense, but a general auction site with antiques, collectibles, ephemera, and a separate category for just postcards.

Buffalo Bid Antique Auction
www.buffalobid.com
All users get free regular listings and free picture uploads. The focus is antiques and collectibles only.

Coy Media Auction
http://www.coymedia.com/auction/
A large site with a bit of everything including hardware, sporting goods, and tickets and travel as well as antiques and collectibles. Self-proclaimed 2nd largest independent online marketplace and auction site in the world.

Debby's Online Auction
http://www.debbys.com
Here's proof that you don't have to be big to have your own auction site. Debby's is a well-designed site with most of the listings from-you guessed it-Debby!

eBay
http://www.ebay.com
The first and the biggest, it is more likely that you will find an item you are looking for than not. eBay™ routinely offers over two million items for sale at any given time, and they are also addressing the online fraud issue by offering insurance on your purchases through Lloyds.

eHammer
http://www.ehammer.com
Offering only antiques and collectibles, eHammer lets you cross-list your items in more than one category, as well as private auction halls to display your items.

Go Main Line
http://www.gomainline.com
A growing site dedicated to just antiques and collectibles. Go Main Line is focusing on quality merchandise and value added services like experts you can contact with your questions about antiques and collectibles.

Haggle Online
http://www.haggle.com
Primarily computers and electronics—if you deal in these items this is one to check out.

Mobilia.com
http://www.mobilia.com
The online home for America's car culture, featuring an online auction and store. Mobilia.com is based in Middlebury, VT and opened for business in February 1999 to provide a centralized community where automobilia enthusiasts can collaborate in discussion and commerce.

Up4Sale Auction
http://www.up4sale.com
Free auctions forever is the motto, and Up4Sale delivers. Toys and Beanies are prolific on this site, but there are other antiques and collectibles too.

ViaBid.com
http://www.viabid.com
Vintage books, autographs, and other antiques and collectibles. ViaBid offers both auctions and fixed price listings, with no listing fees or commissions.

Yahoo! Auctions
http://auctions.yahoo.com
Yahoo! is free to registered users for both buying and selling, and offers you different choices on ending your auctions, including having the auction automatically extend until the bidding stops for a specified period of time, or ending at a fixed time.

Traditional Auction Houses with an Online Presence

Butterfield & Butterfield
http://www.butterfields.com
Recently acquired by eBay™, Butterfield & Butterfield offers live Internet auctions on specific days. You can order a catalog online and fill out a form to place your bid either before the auction starts or during the actual auction—absentee bids are accepted. In addition, there is a Web site feature called Online Collector Magazine, where you can read featured articles by experts, get tips from B&B specialists, and even send a photo of a family heirloom for free appraisal.

Christie's
http://www.christies.com
While there is currently no online auction, Christie's accepts absentee bids for their upcoming regular auctions and the merchandise is available for scrutiny on the site. Auction results are posted by auction date and lot number, so you must have a catalog to gain any benefit from the information. Phone numbers for appraisal specialists are listed—after taking some information from you an estimate of cost is provided before the appraisal is done. All or part of the fee is returned if you should consign your item to Christie's within one year from the date of the appraisal.

Sotheby's
http://www.sothebys.com
Browse an online catalog, or purchase a printed one. Auction results from New York, London, Hong Kong and Geneva are available if you know the auction number (auction numbers are available for upcoming auctions via the online catalog part of the site). A site-specific search engine is available to search for entries with keywords you designate.

Individual Dealers

A-Mark Precious Metals
http://www.amark.com
Since its founding in 1965, A-Mark has grown into a firm with annual sales exceeding $1 billion and is a full service precious metal trading company offering a wide array of products and services. Daily prices are posted for gold, silver and other precious metals.

Hakes Americana & Collectibles
http://www.hakes.com
Hakes mail order auctions are well known in the collectibles trade, and many of the same fine items are available online at fixed prices.

D'Antiques Limited
http://www.dantiques.com
Don't be fooled by the D'Antiques claim of being the premiere virtual junk store on the Web—they have some fine antiques and collectibles too.

Durwyn Smedley Antiques
http://www.smedley.com
Modern design movements of the 20th Century including Arts & Crafts, Art Deco, and Mid-Century Modern. Art pottery and tiles, American designer dinnerware.

Funk and Junk
http://www.funkandjunk.com
Character glasses, action figures, five-and-dime items, political items, vintage clothing, and much more including categories by decades (1950s, 1970's, etc.)

Old Orchard Antiques
http://www.oldorchardantiques.com
A selection of advertising, ephemera, jewelry, glass, pottery, and toys coupled with friendly, efficient service makes this a site to bookmark.

Information Directories

Antique Hot Spots
http://www.antiquehotspots.com
A directory of hundreds of antique and collectibles sites with links to them from one location. You'll find links to anything from online auctions to individual shops to companies where you can buy display showcases.

collect.com
http://www.csmonline.com
Subscribe to the Antique Trader online price guide, plan your next trip with a show and auction calendar, purchase price guides and reference books, join discussion groups, all from one source.

Curioscape
http://www.curioscape.com
A directory of links to specific categories, including art, coins, dolls, glassware, and many more.

Collector Link (Cards)
http://www.collector-link.com
Web sites and news groups for card magazines and price guides, card issuers, dealers and private collectors.

ShopNow.com
http://www.shopnow.com
While this is a site that lists stores of all descriptions, not just antiques and collectibles, all you have to do is type "antiques" or "collectibles" into the Easy-Search box on their home page, click "Find It", and get a list of links to more fun places to explore.

World Collectors Net
http://www.worldcollectorsnet.com
A site for collectibles, featuring a shopping arcade, information pages, articles, reviews, message boards, price guides, a bookstore and a swap shop all under one virtual roof.